Once upon an open book
I dreamed I saw the sun—
It came down to my little house
And stayed 'til day was done.

Once upon an Open Book

Once upon an open book
I dreamed I saw the moon—
It spoke with me from up the sky
And left me all too soon.

Once upon an open book
I dreamed I saw the stars—
They wrapped me in their billion rays
And carried me afar.

—Nancy Bopp

Reading 3 *Part A*
for Christian Schools®
Second Edition

Bob Jones University Press, Greenville, South Carolina 29614

This textbook was written by members of the faculty and staff of Bob Jones University. Standing for the "old-time religion" and the absolute authority of the Bible since 1927, Bob Jones University is the world's leading Fundamentalist Christian university. The staff of the University is devoted to educating Christian men and women to be servants of Jesus Christ in all walks of life.

Providing unparalleled academic excellence, Bob Jones University prepares its students through its offering of over one hundred majors, while its fervent spiritual emphasis prepares their minds and hearts for service and devotion to the Lord Jesus Christ.

If you would like more information about the spiritual and academic opportunities available at Bob Jones University, please call
1-800-BJ-AND-ME (1-800-252-6363).

NOTE:
The fact that materials produced by other publishers may be referred to in this volume does not constitute an endorsement by Bob Jones University Press of the content or theological position of materials produced by such publishers. The position of Bob Jones University Press, and the University itself, is well known. Any references and ancillary materials are listed as an aid to the student or the teacher and in an attempt to maintain the accepted academic standards of the publishing industry.

READING 3A for Christian Schools® Second Edition
Once Upon an Open Book

Produced in cooperation with the Bob Jones University School of Education and Bob Jones Elementary School.

for Christian Schools is a registered trademark of Bob Jones University Press.

Contents

Making Melody

Special Deeds

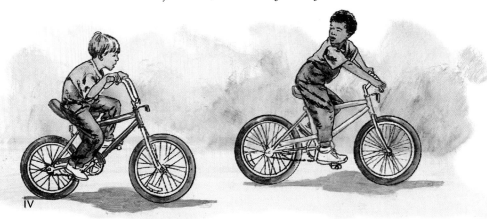

Days to Remember

Acknowledgments

A careful effort has been made to trace the ownership of selections included in this textbook in order to secure permission to reprint copyright material and to make full acknowledgment of their use. If any error or omission has occurred, it is purely inadvertent and will be corrected in subsequent editions, provided written notification is made to the publisher.

Houghton Mifflin Company: Glossary material based on the lexical database of the *Children's Dictionary,* copyright © 1981 Houghton Mifflin Company. No part of this book may be reproduced or transmitted in any form or by any means, electronic or mechanical, including photocopying and recording, or by any information storage or retrieval system, except as may be expressly permitted by the 1976 Copyright Act or with prior written permission from both Houghton Mifflin Company and the Bob Jones University Press.

"Jim" Copyright © 1956 by Gwendolyn Brooks Blakely. Used by permission of HarperCollins Publishers.

Photo Credits

The following agencies and individuals have furnished materials to meet the photographic needs of this textbook. We wish to express our gratitude to them for their important contribution.

Cochlear Corporation
National Aeronautics and Space Administration (NASA)
Ultratec, Inc.
Unusual Films

In the Silent World
Unusual Films 101, 103; Photo courtesy Cochlear Corporation 102; Ultratec, Inc. 104 (both)

Space Walk
NASA 249, 250, 251, 252 (both), 253, 254, 255

Making Melody

The Singing Knight

Becky Davis

illustrated by
Justin Gerard

Sir Bryan

Long, long ago and far away there lived a brave
and handsome knight named Sir Bryan. He wore
shining armor and rode on a sleek white horse named
Charger. Together they would go into battle, Sir Bryan
holding his long spear before him.

Charger would arch his neck and prance forward
proudly whenever Sir Bryan gave a command.

> Then away he would race,
>   faster than sunlight,
>   his mane flowing,
>   his eyes glowing.

Now Sir Bryan could fight just as bravely as any
knight in the whole kingdom. He had done many
brave and knightly deeds.

But still, the other knights did not admire or praise
him. They would look his way and laugh. They
hardly ever spoke to him.

2

Sometimes all the bold knights paraded through a town after a battle. The lovely ladies leaned out their windows. They cheered the brave knights.

When the ladies saw Sir Bryan parading by, they started to cheer him too. But suddenly, one after the other, they opened their eyes wide and gasped. They giggled so hard that they had to hold their scarves over their mouths. Then they turned away from Sir Bryan. They tossed their flowers at the feet of the other knights.

3

The awful truth was that Sir Bryan was different from every other knight. Everyone could see it, even when he wore his whole suit of armor. For Sir Bryan always carried with him a long-necked, stringed lute. Everyone knew that no one who claimed to be a brave knight ever played any sort of musical instrument. Music was played only by bards and jesters!

So no matter how bravely Sir Bryan fought, no one admired him. People only laughed at him because of his lute.

One day, Sir Bryan rode Charger deep into the forest. When he reached a clearing, he said, "This is where we will stop, Charger. I will play my lute in this quiet place."

Sir Bryan sat cross-legged in the grass. He strummed his lute and hummed a sad song to himself.

Charger contentedly munched the grass nearby.
Every once in a while he lifted his head and whinnied.
He sounded as though he felt sad for his master.

"Ah, Charger, my dear friend," Sir Bryan sighed.
"I wish you could tell me what to do. I wish people
would understand. A knight truly can be a brave
knight and like music too. There is really nothing
wrong with putting the two together."

The light, shimmery music of Sir Bryan's lute
always made him feel a little better. For a while he
just strummed and hummed.

"Well, Charger," he finally said, "I know that I
won't give up my lute. So there's just one thing left
to do. I must leave this land. I must find another land
where I can play my lute and be a knight too."

Sir Bryan swung up onto Charger's back. "I must tell the king before I leave," he said. "I will ask him to let me travel to a distant land."

So off Charger galloped,
faster than sunlight,
his mane flowing,
his eyes glowing.

Sir Bryan and Groggle

As Sir Bryan came to the center of town, he saw that the townspeople were in a flurry. A messenger was blowing a horn.

"Hear ye! Hear ye!" the messenger shouted. "The fair Princess Millicent has been captured by the giant Groggle. Any brave and handsome knight who can rescue her will receive a reward. He will be given whatever his heart desires! Hear ye! Hear ye!"

Sir Bryan's heart leaped up within him. His one desire was to be loved and respected by the people of this land. He would fight a giant for that.

Without wasting a moment, Sir Bryan started the quest to rescue Princess Millicent.

Away Charger raced,
faster than sunlight,
his mane flowing,
his eyes glowing.

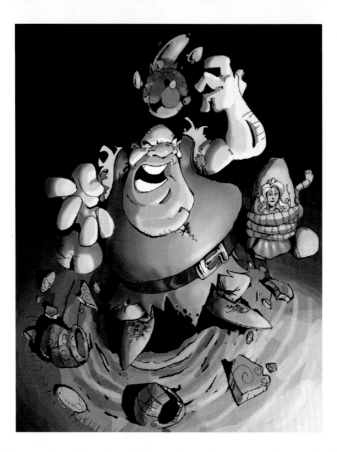

Sir Bryan arrived at the giant's cave long before any of the other knights. Groggle had the lovely Princess Millicent tied to a rock near one side of the cave. He was ranting and raving and throwing things as only a giant can do.

As Sir Bryan reached for his dagger, his hand plucked a few strings of his lute by accident. When Groggle heard the music, he turned around to listen. Sir Bryan strummed the lute again. Groggle stood still.

"It seems that Groggle likes music," Sir Bryan called to Princess Millicent. "Perhaps he is smarter than I thought."

Princess Millicent was too frightened to reply. Sir Bryan kept his eyes on the giant. He put his dagger next to him where he could easily reach it. Then he took his lute and sat cross-legged on Groggle's huge table. He began to play his lute and sing in a soft voice. A lovely tune drifted through the musty air.

Groggle stared and stared. Then he closed his eyes and swayed back and forth as if he were thinking of a lullaby. He stayed that way, even when Sir Bryan put his lute down and cut the cords that bound the princess. Sir Bryan lifted the princess onto Charger's back.

Suddenly Groggle's eyes opened, and he came howling after them. Sir Bryan barely had time to grab his lute. He leaped on Charger's back with Millicent.

Charger raced away,
faster than sunlight,
his mane flowing,
his eyes glowing.

They came to Bottomless River.
Charger took one long leap
over it to the other side.

10

But when clumsy Groggle tried to leap over, he fell into the river with a big splash. He sank all the way to the bottom. And the bottom of the Bottomless River is a long, long way down.

Charger carried Sir Bryan and Princess Millicent back to the palace. The people cheered and shouted. They were all glad that Princess Millicent was home again. And because the giant Groggle was gone, they even cheered Sir Bryan! Sir Bryan bowed and blushed as only a brave and handsome knight can do.

King Edwin said, "Well, my boy, you have brought my daughter back to me. You have shown yourself to be a brave knight. I will reward you by giving you half of my kingdom."

Sir Bryan had received his heart's desire when the people cheered for him, but he thanked the king for his generous reward.

Sir Bryan lived at the palace so that he could rule his half of the kingdom. Soon he and Princess Millicent were married. And so it is told that late in the evening the light, shimmery music of Sir Bryan's lute would float over the castle wall.

And in the moonlight
Charger would toss his head,
his mane flowing,
his eyes glowing.

Music in Your Heart

Eileen Berry

illustrated by
Mary Ann Lumm

Polishing

Marc pulled open the door, and a bell jingled. "Grandfather?"

He breathed deeply. Smells of polish, rosin, and

glue filled the instrument shop as they always did. At a table in one corner, a short, bald man bent over a cello, rubbing a cloth in small circles over the smooth brown wood.

"Marc!" The man glanced up. "Come in, come in. You have finished your lesson, I see."

"Yes," Marc sighed. "My teacher gave me a new piece to learn for the school recital." Marc stood behind his grandfather's left shoulder, watching.

Grandfather turned to face him. "Let me see your violin."

Marc handed him the instrument. Grandfather turned the violin over in his hands, and his careful eyes studied it through his little round glasses. "It needs polishing," he said. He pulled up another chair and tossed Marc a cloth. "Make it shine."

The two worked quietly for a while. Marc listened to the whisking sounds of cloth on wood, sounds as soft as breathing.

"This takes a long time, doesn't it, Grandfather?"

Grandfather smiled. "Polishing?" He chuckled. "Yes, polishing takes a fair amount of time. But clean wood gives a clean sound. Always remember that."

Marc nodded. He had heard his grandfather say those words many times.

"This recital—when is it?" asked Grandfather.

"In two months," said Marc.

"Not long to learn a piece."

"No."

"You will have some polishing to do—of another kind."

Marc thought of the little upstairs room with the window where he practiced, and his shoulders slumped. Every day after school he played his violin there for an hour. Sometimes his mother played the piano along with him. But even then, the minutes crept by slowly.

"Grandfather, do you still practice every day?"

Grandfather did not answer just then. Instead, he lowered the cello gently to the floor between his knees. He picked up the bow, closed his eyes, and played a melody—a low and beautiful one that made Marc think of the wind sighing through the pines at night.

"I still play a little every day," the old man said finally. "I cannot help it. Music has gotten into my heart, and if I didn't let the song come out somehow, my heart would burst."

He stood and placed the cello back on the table. Then he took off his glasses, wiped the back of his hand across his eyes, put the glasses on again, and bent to his polishing.

"How do you get music into your heart?" Marc asked. He leaned forward eagerly.

Grandfather gave his chuckle again. "It puts itself there," he said, "as you polish."

Marc frowned and went on rubbing his cloth over the wood of his violin, watching for the shine he knew would come.

Shining

Marc's friend Paul kicked the soccer ball to him. "Can you stay a while longer?" he asked. "Some of the guys want to stay after soccer practice and play another game."

Marc strung his soccer cleats over one shoulder and faced Paul. "I can't stay," he said. "Maybe next week. But not today. I've got to practice violin."

"But it will be for only an hour or so," said Paul. "We need you to make a team." He bounced the ball off his knee.

Marc looked out at the field where the boys were gathering. Then he looked across the street toward his house. What would it matter if he missed one day of violin practice? Then he thought of his grandfather and the melody he had played on the cello in his shop.

"I can't, Paul," he said. "I have to learn my recital piece by heart."

"Okay," said Paul, "if that's what you want." He ran off toward the field.

Marc's throat felt tight. He swallowed and turned quickly toward his house. In the quiet upstairs room, he took his violin out of its case. He stood in front of the window and began to play. From where he stood, he could see the other boys running and kicking the ball on the soccer field. Marc pulled down the shade with a snap and laid his violin aside.

A footstep sounded behind him. He whirled around. Mother stood in the doorway.

"Your grandfather—my father—always hated to practice," she said.

Marc looked at the floor. "But Grandfather loves to practice. Music is in his heart. He said so."

Mother smiled. "It hasn't always been that way. Not when he was a boy growing up in Poland. A family friend gave him the violin and taught him a little. But your grandfather was much more interested in the outdoors, working in the fields with his brothers and playing rough-and-tumble games.

"When he first came to America, jobs were hard to find. Before long he realized that his violin was his only means of earning a living. So with the little he knew, he played on street corners, in hotels, in parks—wherever he could find work."

Mother sat down on the piano bench. "The more your grandfather played because he *had* to, the more he realized that he *wanted* to. As time went by, music became so much a part of him that he wanted to work with it always. His dream was to be a concert violinist. But he had a family to feed by that time and no money for music training. So he opened his instrument shop. Sometimes people traded with him. He would repair their instruments, and they would teach him. That's how he learned."

Mother leaned forward and gave Marc's shoulder a soft squeeze. "Be thankful," she said, "that you can have lessons."

Mother left. Marc sat quietly, thinking, while the clock ticked. Then he stood, laid out his music on the stand, and picked up his violin again.

At last the day of the recital came. That morning, Marc sat alone in his practice room and polished his violin. As he rubbed the cloth over the instrument, he remembered Grandfather's words: "Clean wood gives a clean sound."

Behind the stage of the school auditorium, Marc tuned his violin and played a few notes of his piece. Yes, it sounded clean.

Marc walked onto the stage, tucked his violin under his chin, and lifted the bow. The first notes eased their way into the air, clear and pure. Marc felt a smile curving up the corners of his mouth. He suddenly remembered Grandfather's melody that had sounded like wind in the pines. He closed his eyes and played on by heart to the end.

As the last note died away, the audience began to clap. Marc bowed and looked out into the crowd. Someone at the back was standing, clapping hard. It was Grandfather.

Marc bowed again. His mouth felt stretched to its limit with smiling.

Mother hurried to Marc after the recital. "Grandfather said to tell you he was sorry," she said. "He couldn't stay. But he wanted me to give you this."

She handed Marc a recital program that listed each piece and the names of the students who had played. Beside Marc's name, Grandfather had scribbled a note.

"Dear Marc," it read, "Somehow you have gotten music into your heart. Once it happens, it lasts forever. But remember, my boy, the way to keep shining is to keep polishing. And always remember—clean wood gives a clean sound. Grandfather."

TRUMPETS AND PITCHERS

*Karen Wilt / illustrated by
Del Thompson and Johanna Berg*

(based on Judges 6-7)

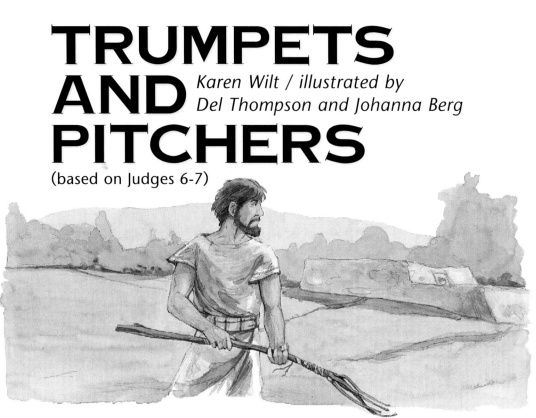

Because the children of Israel had turned from God, He sent the powerful Midianite army to trouble them. Judges 6 and 7 tell the story of the godly young man chosen by God to lead Israel back to Him and then to victory over the enemy.

Gideon's Trumpet Call

Gideon stopped to rest. He looked at the pile of wheat left to thresh. He dared not rest long. The wheat must be threshed and hidden from the enemy. Then Gideon's family would have wheat to make bread. They would not go hungry. Gideon stretched and looked around. No one was in sight.

He walked back to the piles of wheat by the winepress.

As he passed an oak tree, a voice said, "The Lord is with you. You are a brave man."

Gideon turned around quickly. He peered into the shadows under the tree. "The Lord has forsaken us and given us into the hands of the enemy," Gideon said quietly.

"You will save your people from the enemy. Have I not sent you?" the man said.

"Please do not go away," said Gideon.

He ran to prepare an offering. He made some cakes and sacrificed a goat. Gideon brought his offering back to the oak tree. Carefully he placed it on a rock. The man held out his staff, and the sacrifice burst into flames. Then Gideon knew that this man was an angel of the Lord.

Gideon stepped back and fell to his knees, but the angel of the Lord had left as suddenly as he had come.

That same night the Lord spoke to Gideon again. He told Gideon to destroy his father's altar and to cut down the idols beside it. He told Gideon to make an altar to the Lord God.

But Gideon feared the people of his father's household and of the city. They would be angry if he cut down their idols. So Gideon waited. After dark, he took ten servants and slipped out to do as God had commanded.

In the morning a huge crowd gathered. "Who did this?" the people murmured. "Who cut down our idols?"

"It was Gideon," someone called out.

The crowd rushed to Gideon's house. "Send Gideon out," they shouted. "We will kill him!"

Gideon's father opened the door. "Will you plead for your idols?" he asked. "If your idols are so great, let them plead for themselves. Those who worship them should be killed. They have sinned against the Lord God."

Not far away, in the Valley of Jezreel, Gideon watched the enemy soldiers gather. They came from the east and the south. Their tents filled the valley.

Gideon took out his trumpet and blew a call to war. Men came to join him.

Other men ran with the news to far-off places. They told how Gideon had destroyed the idols and planned to fight the enemy. Soon an army of men came to help Gideon.

Then Gideon talked to God again. He wanted the army to see that God would give them the victory. He wanted to know that he was doing just as God wanted.

"Will You save Your people as You have said?" he asked. "I will put a sheepskin on the ground. If it is wet with dew and the ground is dry, then I will know that You are going to save Your people."

Gideon set the sheepskin on the ground. Then he went to bed. When morning came, Gideon hurried to check the sheepskin. The ground was dry all around the sheepskin, but the sheepskin glistened and sparkled in the morning sunlight. It started to drip as Gideon lifted it. He wrung a bowlful of water out of it!

Gideon prayed again. "Do not be angry," he said, "but once more show Your power. This time let the sheepskin be dry and the ground be wet with dew."

Gideon left the sheepskin out again. The night stretched on and on.

When the first light of morning shone, Gideon sprang up to check the sheepskin. He ran through the wet grass and scooped the sheepskin up. It was dry! The Lord God was going to save His people from the enemy.

The Battle of the Lord

As the army marched, the Lord spoke to Gideon. "The people are too many. They will think they have won the battle themselves. Tell those who are afraid of the battle to go home."

Gideon followed the Lord's command. Twenty-two thousand men admitted that they were afraid and went home. Only ten thousand men stayed.

Then the Lord spoke to Gideon again. "There are still too many people," He said.

Gideon took the army to get a drink at the stream. The men had marched for days on hot, dusty roads. They were tired and thirsty. Many of them fell on their knees or bent over to drink the cool water.

Others scooped up handfuls of water and lapped it like thirsty dogs. They watched the hills for the enemy as they drank the cool water.

"Keep the ones that lapped the water," said the Lord. "Send the others home."

Only three hundred men had lapped the water. Gideon's army looked very small.

That night, Gideon and his servant crept down to the Valley of Jezreel. The enemy soldiers covered the valley like a swarm of grasshoppers. Even their camels were too many to be counted.

"Our army is so small," whispered Gideon. "The enemy has many more men than we have."

The servant touched Gideon's arm and pointed. Two men were walking toward them. Gideon and his servant stepped behind some rocks and stood very still. The men kept on walking and talking.

"I dreamed a dream," one said. "A huge cake of barley bread tumbled into our camp, crushing it flat. Look, my hands are still shaking. It was an awful nightmare."

The other man shook his head in despair. "That barley cake must mean Gideon. His God will deliver us into his hand."

Gideon and his servant slipped quietly away. "The Lord God is fighting for us. Hurry, let us wake up our army," Gideon said.

Quickly Gideon prepared the army. Each man was given a trumpet and an empty pitcher. Bright torches were placed inside the pitchers.

Gideon's voice rang out over the camp. "Look at me!" he commanded. "When we come to the camp of the enemy, do as I do."

Then all was silent except the tramp, tramp, tramp of marching feet.

The little army surrounded the camp. The dark night hid the waiting men well.

Gideon blew his trumpet mightily. The army took up the sound, each man on his own trumpet. Gideon broke his pitcher and let his torch shine. The army broke their pitchers. All the torches shone! The enemy camp was circled by a ring of fire!

Gideon shouted. The army shouted with him. But not one man lifted a hand to fight.

The Lord confused the enemy. They began to fight each other. They fled back and forth within the camp.

Gideon and his men watched as the enemy began to flee. "Look," called Gideon. "The enemy army is running away! The Lord God has saved His people!"

Then Gideon raised his trumpet again. He blew another loud blast.

Together Gideon and his men ran toward the enemy camp.

Together they chased out the last of the enemy.

O sing unto the Lord a new song; for he hath done marvellous things: his right hand, and his holy arm, hath gotten him the victory. (Psalm 98:1)

An Instrument for God

Maggie D. Sloan / illustrated by John Roberts

In the mid-1900s, John and Isobel Kuhn and their daughter Kathryn traveled as missionaries to the Lisu, a group of people who lived in a remote part of China. Knowing about the Lisu's love for music, Isobel brought along a portable organ. This story is based on the "baby organ" Isobel brought and how she used it in her ministry to the Lisu.

On the Trail

Isobel and Kathryn stopped at the top of a steep trail. Before them, rugged mountain peaks rose out of the clouds. Deep, dark canyons were also etched into the landscape. Isobel's heart beat faster as she pointed them out to her daughter. She squeezed Kathryn's hand.

"Look, Kathryn!" she said. "The Salween River flows in one of those dark canyons, and the Lisu people live along that river!"

Isobel's husband, John, stood a few feet away from them. Soon he turned and walked back to where Isobel and Kathryn were standing. "It won't be long now," he said. Isobel could see the excitement in his blue eyes. John, too, had been waiting for this moment.

John frowned. "But the trip going down is not going to be easy. The mules will really have a hard time," he said.

Isobel was worried. What if someone were hurt or even killed? She looked at the mules packed with their belongings. What if everything they had brought were lost? One mule carrying a black box caught her eye. What about her "baby organ"? It was a gift from the Christian girls at the Corner Club. Isobel knew the Lisu people loved music. How could she teach them new songs without it?

Then the Lord spoke to Isobel's heart. "Trust Me," He said.

Isobel was ashamed. She prayed, "Lord, please forgive me. Help me to trust You more."

The next afternoon, an unhappy muleteer walked over to where John was standing. "It is too dangerous," he said. "We must go back and find a safer way."

Isobel could not believe what she was hearing. There was not enough food to go back, and it would mean a further delay in getting to the Lisu people.

"You must try," John said. "Lighten the load and take two trips if you have to."

The muleteer left, shaking his head. Isobel knew he did not agree with John's plan.

As they passed each dangerous place where a landslide had covered the trail, Isobel prayed, "Lord, please keep everyone and everything safe with each crossing."

That night, Isobel, John, and Kathryn reached the canyon of the Salween River. Isobel was very happy. They were spending the night in Lisu country!

The next afternoon, Isobel's heart was a little heavy when John led Kathryn and her to their new home.

Cold air greeted Isobel when she stepped inside the gloomy, deserted hut. The only sign of life was a scrap of yellowed paper hanging on a wall. There was nothing else. The pack mules had not arrived yet. What if all were lost?

The paper drew Isobel's attention. It read, *My God shall supply all your need*. "Oh, Lord," she prayed, "please forgive me for not trusting You enough. Help me to trust You to supply *all* our needs."

Eldest Sister

A few days later, the pack mules and muleteer arrived. Looking over the loads, Isobel brightened at the sight of a black box. The "baby organ" had survived!

A group of curious Lisu gathered when the organ was moved into the little church. A black box that turned into an instrument! When Isobel played for them, there was a reverent silence. Then one by one, rich voices joined the mellow notes of the organ.

One Sunday morning, Isobel noticed a new girl in the congregation. It was Eldest Sister, the lovely and shy girl Isobel had seen often in the village. She knew Eldest Sister and her family were not Christians. The girl's eyes were fixed on John as he preached. Every once in a while she looked thoughtful.

Isobel hoped to talk with Eldest Sister after the service, but the girl left as soon as the service ended.

Week after week, Eldest Sister came to church. Every time she left as soon as it was over. John, Isobel, and Kathryn prayed faithfully for the girl.

One Monday evening Isobel stopped reading when she heard someone knocking at the door.

"Who could that be at this time of the night?" she asked John.

John went to see. Eldest Sister stood outside. "I heard the music from the organ. I came to church to learn what the songs were about," she said. "Please, I want to become a Christian."

John and Isobel showed her some verses. Eldest Sister nodded. She understood. Isobel could hardly keep back tears of joy as the girl prayed. Eldest Sister accepted Jesus as her Savior.

Isobel hugged Eldest Sister. "Thank you, Ma-ma and Pa-pa," Eldest Sister said. She addressed John and Isobel just as the other Lisu believers did. "Thank you for showing me how to become a Christian."

That night Isobel thought about what Eldest Sister had said. The songs from the organ had brought her to church. "Thank you, Lord," Isobel prayed, "for making my 'baby organ' an instrument for You."

Song Signals

Karen Wooster

illustrated by
Steve Christopher

Have you ever stopped to listen to the songs of the birds? Each kind of bird sings its own special song. If you listen carefully to the song, you may be able to identify the singing bird.

Most often birds sing calls to their own families. Birds attract their mates by singing. Early in the spring, the birds' songs begin. When a bird finds a mate, the two fly off to find a home. There they sing to protect their home, warning other birds to stay away.

Sometimes it seems that birds sing because they are happy. Their songs seem to praise God. The twittering "cheep, cheep, cheep" of a house sparrow adds cheer to bleak winter days. All year round the joyful "teakettle, teakettle" song of the Carolina wren can be heard.

The cries of the songbird are different from its singing. The cries are used to signal the flock, warn others, or call for help.

When the catbird senses danger, it interrupts its song with a catlike cry. The "mew, mew" warns the other birds to leave. Some brave birds aren't fooled by the catbird's signal, and they don't fly away. Then a fight often occurs to decide which bird will stay.

Have you ever seen sparrows all leave a tree at the same time? They are obeying a signal to leave. Birds use many cries to inform the flock. These cries are their signals.

The sharp cry of alarm may be given by any bird. Blue jays are an excellent alarm for other animals. The blue jays may warn forest animals of a hunter. Their sharp cries may also reveal a cat stalking a sparrow.

There are certain birds whose songs are really copies of other birds' songs. It seems as if they like to tease and mimic others. A blue jay may copy the songs of the catbird or the wren. Then there are times when its shriek of "jay, jay, jay" teases a cat.

The master mimic is the mockingbird. The Indians called this bird "four hundred tongues." It is able to make its songs sound like the songs of many other birds. The mockingbird also mimics other sounds. Its song may even sound like a flute or a whistle.

Listen carefully to the birds' songs. Can you tell what their signals mean?

Whistles

Dorothy Aldis

illustrated by Kathy Pflug

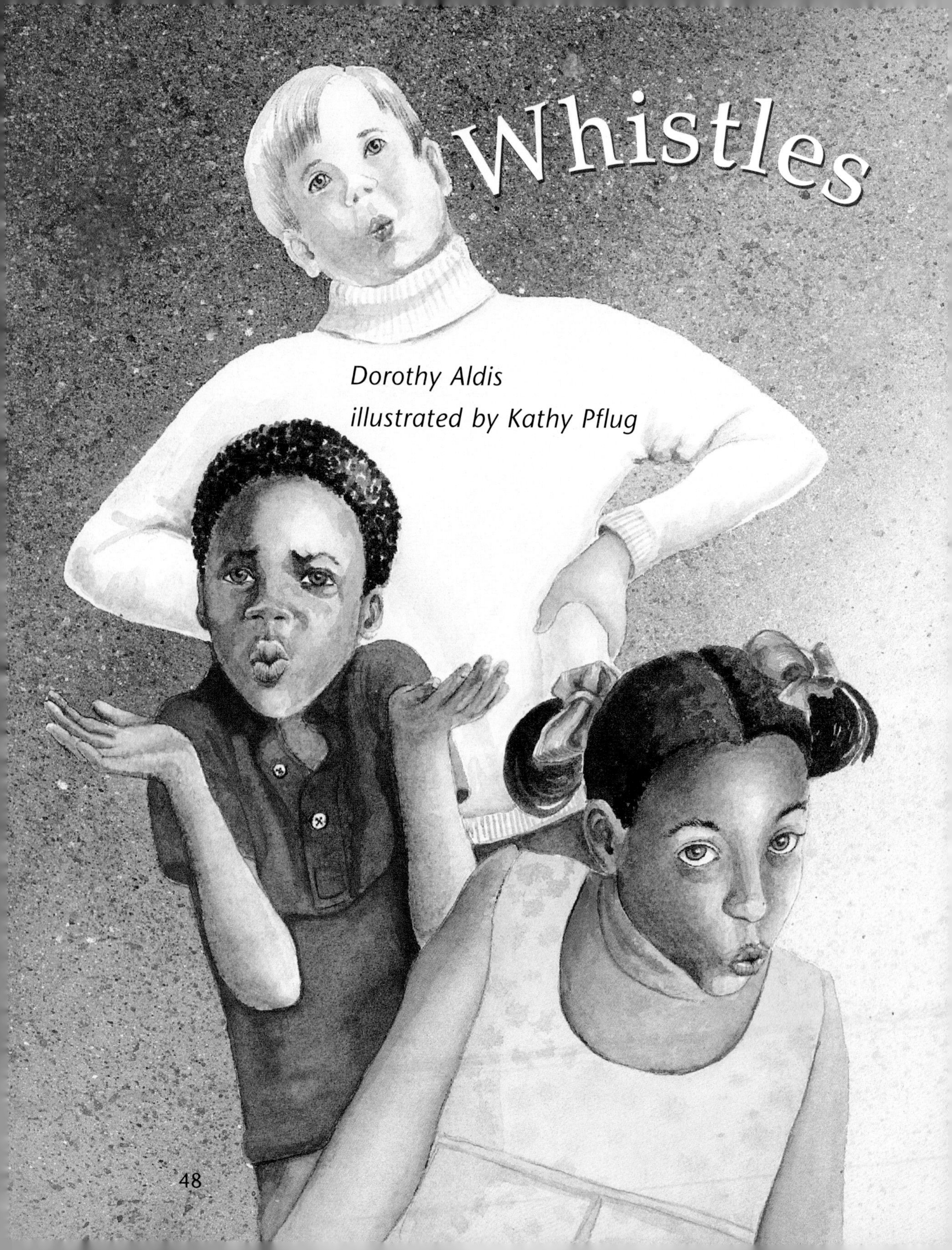

I want to learn to whistle,
I've always wanted to.
I fix my mouth to do it, but
The whistle won't come through.

I think perhaps it's stuck, and so
I try it once again.
Can people swallow whistles?
Where is my whistle then?

The Coyote's Song

Karen Wooster and Rebecca Fitchner
illustrated by Stephanie True and Johanna Berg

Have you ever had trouble remembering something? In this adaptation of a traditional Native American tale, the coyote cannot remember a song, no matter how hard he tries!

Cast	Coyote	Gopher	Pigeons	Narrator
	Locust	Crow	Fish	

Act I

Narrator: Long ago there lived a coyote on the plains. At the edge of the plains was the forest. There, in a tall tree, lived a locust. Each morning the coyote left his home and family to go hunting in the forest. Each morning the singing locust sat on the branch of his tall tree. One day while the coyote was hunting, he passed the tree and heard the locust's song.

50

Coyote: *(looking up)* Who is singing such beautiful music?

Locust: How kind you are! Tell me, is the song really as lovely as you say?

Coyote: Oh, yes! Won't you teach it to me? My family would like to hear your song.

Locust:
Very well. Listen carefully while I sing it again.

Narrator: The coyote listened. Then he tried to sing the song. But it was the locust's song, and coming from the coyote, it sounded a little scratchy.

Locust: Well, that sounds pretty good for the first try. But why don't you sing your own song?

Coyote: Oh, yours sounds much better, and I'll learn it in no time.

Locust: Very well. Let's try again.

Coyote: I know it well enough now. I can almost hear it in my mind. I'll go and sing it to my family.

Narrator: The coyote turned and started home. He was so busy singing to himself that he didn't watch where he was going.

Crow: *(cawing)* Beware, beware!

Narrator: The coyote stepped into a gopher's hole, and down he went! Dust flew everywhere.

Coyote: *(angrily accusing)* Gopher, you have made this path nothing but holes and dusty traps!

Gopher: *(peering out of a hole in the path)* You were not watching where you were going, Coyote.

Crow: Caw! Caw! You had your head in the air.

Gopher: Yes, what were you doing?

Coyote: *(scrambling to his feet)* I was singing a beautiful song, and you have made me lose it!

Narrator: The coyote scratched his head. He thought and thought, but he couldn't remember the locust's song.

Coyote:
I suppose
I'll have to go
back to Locust. He will
sing the song again for me.

Crow: Caw! Caw! I have a song for you.

Coyote: Well, all right. Let's hear it then.

Narrator: The crow sang his song, and the coyote sat with his head cocked, listening. Almost before the crow stopped singing, the coyote jumped up.

Coyote: That's an interesting song! I like it even more than the locust's song. My family will love it.

Act II

Narrator: The coyote started home again, singing the crow's song as he trotted along the trail. He was so proud of his new song that he sang it very loudly. But it was the crow's song, and coming from a coyote, it sounded a little scary.

Pigeons: *(fluttering out of the tall grass along the trail)* Coo! Coo! Don't startle us so!

Coyote: *(falling backward)* Oh, you silly birds. You have frightened the song right out of my head! I won't be able to take it home to my family.

Pigeons: Coo! What song?

Coyote: Why, the song I was singing, you silly birds—the crow's song.

Pigeons: Coo! The crow's song is gone! Why don't you sing your own song?

Coyote: I wanted to take a wonderful song back with me to my children.

Pigeons: *(fluttering overhead)* Coo! Why not learn our song? We'll teach you to sing like us.

Narrator: The pigeons sang their song. The coyote listened closely.

Coyote: Now that's a thrilling song. That's the one I'll sing for my family. It's the best of all. Thank you, pigeons.

Narrator: The coyote left for home, practicing as he went. But the song was the pigeons' song, and coming from the coyote, it sounded a little squeaky.

Pigeons: Coo! Coo! It doesn't go like that!

Narrator: The coyote kept on singing and running. He didn't want to lose the song this time! He ran past another of gopher's holes.

Gopher: *(ducking his head)* Watch out! You're kicking dust into my home!

Narrator: The coyote only ran faster. It was getting dark. He could barely see the path in the darkness. At last he came to a stream. He tried to jump the stream, but in the darkness, he misjudged how far he had to jump. Into the stream he fell.

Coyote: *(sputtering to the fish swimming around him)* Out of my way, out of my way!

Fish: Watch out! You are getting our water muddy!

Coyote: Muddy water! That is the least of my troubles. I've forgotten my song again, and now I have no song to sing to my family.

Act III

Narrator: Wet and tired, the coyote trotted through the darkness toward home.

Coyote: What will I do? I have wasted my whole day, and I still don't have a song to sing to my little ones.

Crow: Caw!

Coyote: Oh, Crow! What will I do?

Crow: Just sing the song you know.

Coyote: Well, I guess I'll have to since it's the only one I have.

Narrator: The coyote began to sing. And since it was the coyote's song, coming from the coyote, it sounded just the way it was meant to sound. Above him the roosting pigeons sang softly. The locust heard the song from his tree and smiled.

Crow: Now, that is the best song I've ever heard you sing.

Coyote: Thank you all! And thank you, Crow! Now, will you go home with me and help me sing to my family? You can sing your song, and I'll sing mine.

Crow: Caw! Caw!

Narrator: The coyote and the crow started down the path, the coyote trotting along and the crow flapping above him. And as they went, each one sang his own song. When they passed the gopher's hole, the gopher stuck out his head.

Gopher: *(yawning)* Why, that *is* a pretty song, Coyote.

Narrator: He ducked back inside his hole, sleepily humming. The coyote trotted down the hill and splashed across the stream.

Fish: *(blowing bubbles)* We like your song too, Coyote.

Narrator: The fish began to sing quietly. The coyote smiled. On the other side of the stream, he stopped to look up at the crow.

Crow: *(softly)* Caw! Caw!

Coyote: *(softly)* O-O-OOO!

61

The Amazing *Mozart*

unattributed

illustrated by Johanna Berg

On January 27, 1756, Leopold
Mozart, the archbishop's musician,
held his newborn son in his arms.
As he hummed a lullaby and rocked
Wolfgang to sleep, Herr Mozart
must have wondered whether his
son would become a musician like himself. He never guessed that
his little baby son would someday write over six hundred pieces
of music and be remembered all over the world.

An Amazing Child

Maria Anna Mozart
finished practicing for her
lesson. She put her music
book away and left the
harpsichord. Quickly,
three-year-old
Wolfgang climbed
onto the bench.
He began to play
the notes he
had heard.

Even when he was three, Wolfgang knew that some notes sounded nice together. He knew that others sounded bad. If he played notes that sounded bad, his eyes filled with tears. But when his melodies sounded nice, he was so excited that he would call his family to come and listen.

By the time Wolfgang was four, he could play many melodies. Sometimes he would play an entire piece from memory.

By the age of five, he was even writing some of his own music!

One day Wolfgang's papa brought some of his musician friends home. They found Wolfgang working hard over a piece of paper.

"I wrote this to play on the harpsichord," said Wolfgang, holding up the paper.

Papa smiled as he looked at the messy paper. Wolfgang had found it hard to write without dripping and spilling the ink. But he had no trouble with the music itself.

"See here," said Papa to his friends. "It is all written correctly. But it is very difficult. No one will be able to play it."

Wolfgang went to the harpsichord to play his music. But even though he could hear the music in his mind, it was so hard he could play only parts of it.

Wolfgang's gift for making music included more than the harpsichord. He also liked to play the violin. When Wolfgang was six, he was given a violin as a present.

One evening Papa and two friends sat down to practice. They were playing some new melodies for stringed instruments. Wolfgang asked if he could play the part of the second violin. But Papa shook his head. He had not taught Wolfgang to play the violin.

Papa's friends saw that the little boy was disappointed. One of the friends suggested that Wolfgang play the second part along with him.

"All right," Papa finally agreed. "You may play, Wolfgang. But you must play so softly that no one can hear you."

When the music was finished, tears were running
down Papa's cheeks. Wolfgang had played the part
perfectly.

An Accomplished Composer

Mozart's father knew that it was time to share his children's talents with people outside their hometown. He began to take his son and daughter to other cities. There, others could enjoy their music.

In almost every country the Mozarts visited, the children performed for the king and queen. Everyone enjoyed hearing them play. Wolfgang could play the harpsichord without a mistake, even when the keyboard was covered with a cloth!

In the city of Vienna, the children played for the emperor and empress. Maria Anna and Wolfgang pleased all who listened. The empress was even more charmed when small Wolfgang climbed on her lap and kissed her.

When Wolfgang was fourteen, he and his father visited the city of Rome. There they went to hear a special song. Only those who sang the marvelous song were allowed to see the music. Anyone who tried to copy the music would be punished.

Wolfgang listened carefully to the music. When he went home that night, he wrote the entire song from memory. The people of Rome were amazed that a young boy had been able to remember and write the song. They were so surprised that they forgot to punish him! Instead, they went to his concerts to hear the talented boy play.

In Rome, Wolfgang was invited to become a member of a special music club. To become a member, he had to take a special test. The test was very hard. It had never been given to anyone under twenty years old. But fourteen-year-old Wolfgang finished the test in much less time than anyone else had ever done! All the judges agreed that Wolfgang Mozart should become a member of their club.

Wolfgang kept writing music. He wrote and wrote, night and day. He wrote beautiful operas and other kinds of music.

It wasn't until after Mozart died that he became famous for his written music. Then people began to enjoy the music he had written, like "The Magic Flute."

Today we no longer remember him as Mozart, the amazing child, but as Mozart, the composer.

A Song in the Night

Dawn L. Watkins / illustrated by Mary Ann Lumm

More than a hundred years ago, it was legal for people to buy and sell other people as slaves. Zoe, a slave born of slave parents, begins to understand the risks of a life like hers.

Poor Wayfarin' Stranger

Zoe sat as close to the fire as she dared. The light from it was small. But the hearth stones were at least a little warm.

Her grandmother held Zoe's baby brother. She hummed a tune. Zoe knew it well: "I'm Just a Poor Wayfarin' Stranger."

She liked it when the sun went down and Grandmother hummed.

The door scraped across the dirt floor, and in came Zoe's father. His shirt was dirty; he smelled of the horses he tended. He sat down slowly on the bed by the wall. But no matter how tired he was, he winked at Zoe and said, "Hello, Light."

And Zoe, no matter what had happened during the day, smiled at her father. "Hello, Papa."

Grandmother laid the baby on a pile of soft cloths by the hearth. She got up and poured some soup into a bowl and handed it to her son.

He bowed his head, and Zoe waited. Behind her the last piece of wood burned through. It fell into the ashes with a little sigh.

"Papa," Zoe said. He looked over at her. "What happened to Zekial's papa?"

Her father winced. He stopped spooning soup. He looked past her to his mother. Grandmother sat down and took up the baby, but she did not hum.

"What do you be knowing about that?" her father said.

"I heard he be dead."

"That's so."

"But how, Papa?"

Her father ate the rest of his meal without answering. Then he set down his bowl and held out his arms. Zoe got into his lap. He folded his big arms about her. She smelled the horses again.

"Little Light," he said, "Zekial's papa, he die like a man. A bad man kill him for nothing."

She looked at the fire. "I heard he try to run."

Her father breathed a big breath. "No." He pulled her tighter to him. "He only say he might run."

"Why?" She wanted her father to make everything right with his words. Papa could do that.

"His life been bad, Light. His baby die. His wife be taken away. His master wicked to him." Her father rocked her side to side.

"Master Jack?"

Her father said nothing.

Zoe asked, "Where Zekial now?"

"I don't know, Baby. I don't know."

Her grandmother said, "Hush, Zoe. Your Papa worn out."

Zoe leaned back against her father. He tipped his head against hers. A tear, like a tiny drop of rain, hit her hand. She sat very still, for she had never seen her father cry.

Grandmother started to hum again. Then she sang in a quiet, husky voice. "I'm just a poor wayfarin' stranger, a-travelin' through this world of woe."

This World of Woe

Sometime in the night, Zoe's mother came in. She never scraped the door the way her father did. But Zoe heard her anyway. She stepped over to the baby. In the little light from the coals, she stroked his face. When he wiggled, she picked him up and cuddled him to her.

Zoe felt good in her quilt. Her father breathed his sleeping breaths. Grandmother slept solid behind her. Then she thought of Zekial. Was he warm? Did he have enough soup?

Her mother carried the baby to bed with her. She got in beside Papa. He stirred a bit. Then all was quiet. Zoe nearly fell back to sleep.

"What?" Papa said, very low.

Her mother caught a little sob. "I heard talk," she said.

Zoe held her breath. She did not even blink.

"Talk?" her father said.

"About you, Lucius."

"About what?"

Her mother struggled down another sob. The baby whimpered.

"Tradin' you to Master Jack."

Zoe's heart stopped. Master Jack had killed Zekial's father. Why would he want Papa?

Her mother cried. Her father said, "Hush, hush," like he always told Zoe when she cried. And then the crying was muffled. Zoe could not see, but she knew Papa had his big arms around Mama.

Light came through the cracks in the door. Zoe sat up. Papa and Mama's bed was empty. Grandmother and the baby were gone too. Zoe sprang up, her heart pounding.

She pulled the door open and ran out. The morning was bright. But there was a little white frost on things. Her mother was sweeping the back porch of the big house. Grandmother was gathering up wood for the fire, the baby in one arm.

Zoe ran barefooted to her grandmother. "Where Papa?"

"There." Grandmother pointed.

Her father was leading a team of horses from the stable.

Grandmother said, "Get inside, child. In your nightdress!"

Zoe made little leaping hops back to the cabin. Had she dreamed all that in the night? She leaned out the door to see her mother again. She swept as though the porch were thick with mud. Whoosh! Whoosh!

Grandmother pushed by with sticks in one arm and the baby in the other. Zoe moved back into the cabin and closed the door.

As she pulled on her shift, she said, "You hear Mama last night?"

Grandmother said, "Here—your bread."

Zoe did not take the bread. "And her crying? You hear that?"

Grandmother said, "Your folks need to be naming this baby."

Zoe stomped her foot. "Mama said Papa be traded!"

"No such thing." Grandmother plopped her down on the one chair in the room. "Now eat."

Zoe looked at her and then toward the door. No, she had not been dreaming. Mama had said what she had said.

Zoe cracked the door again and looked out. Her father's voice carried on the crisp air. He was singing!

A-Travelin' Through

Zoe stayed awake that night. No one had said that anything was different. But Zoe could tell.

Papa had not come in at all that day. Mama had come many times. And her grandmother had done more baking than she did even on a holiday.

At supper, Papa had prayed a long time for all their friends on the other places. Zoe looked from face to face as he prayed. Mama's mouth was straight. Papa raised his eyebrows as he talked.

Grandmother rocked a little in her chair and mumbled to herself. Suddenly she opened one eye and peered at Zoe. Zoe closed her eyes and ducked her chin.

Papa tucked her in early, with another long prayer. Zoe wanted to ask him what was different. But something deep in her said not to.

At last, Mama came in. She went to the fire. Grandmother still sat there holding the baby. Zoe's father sat up and looked at his wife.

Mama nodded. "True," she said. "The missus say so."

Papa went to her and put his arms around her. "Go down, Moses."

Zoe nearly asked out loud what he meant by that. But before she could, he kissed her mother and then came toward her.

"Light," he said.

She sat up and reached for him. He lifted her and whispered in her ear. "We just some poor, wayfarin' strangers. Now not a word, my baby."

Zoe's mother made her put on both her shifts, one over the other. Then she wrapped the baby in two long blankets. Grandmother wrapped Zoe's feet in strips of cloth. And very low she was humming.

Papa carried Zoe and Mama carried the baby. Grandmother had a big basket on one arm and a bundle tied at her side. Together they all went out into the night. The stars were bright as lanterns.

At first light, they stopped. Papa found a hollow in the side of a hill. They all got in and he pulled some brush in front of them. Grandmother gave everyone a piece of bread.

Zoe said, "I'm thirsty."

Mama stroked Zoe's chin. "Shhhh. After while."

When dark came again, they walked again.

Near morning, Papa set Zoe down, put his finger to his lips, and walked away. Zoe's mother held the baby so close that Zoe wondered how he breathed.

Papa returned and waved for them to come on. Zoe ran to him—and stopped. Beyond him stood a white man. But Papa smiled. He said softly, "Friend."

Night after night they walked. Every day but one they hid in someone's barn or attic. Mama cried sometimes when she thought Zoe was asleep.

Then late one night, ahead of them in the woods, a man was singing. "I'm just a poor wayfarin' stranger."

"Praise the Lord," said Grandmother. "Praise the Lord."

The singing got louder as they got closer. Then there stood a black man, with a lantern and a smile.

Papa walked right up to him. "Moses?"

The man nodded. "You on free soil, brother."

Zoe's mother started to cry. The baby whimpered.

That night they slept in a house. They slept a long, long time.

"Light, wake up," said her mother. Mama hardly ever called her that. But Mama was smiling big this morning.

Zoe went out into the sunlight. Everyone turned to her.

"This be Light," Papa said. "That her real name. And this," he said, holding up the baby, "be Freedom."

Zoe looked at her brother as though she had never seen him before. Then in a rich voice, her grandmother started to sing. "I'm just a-goin' over Jordan." One by one, they all joined her: "I'm just a-goin' over home."

Special Deeds

The Spelling Window

Dawn L. Watkins

illustrated by John Roberts

Part I

Seth has blond hair like Kathy and me. And he would be in Kathy's grade, except he goes to a special school downtown. He points at pictures and brings them to us. And he spells on his fingers and talks with his hands.

My sister Kathy can spell on her fingers too. She and Seth can spell across the alley between our apartments because we have a window that is even with Seth's window. I know a few things they say, but I don't spell on my fingers.

One day when it poured down rain, Kathy tried to make Seth see her words at the spelling window, but she couldn't. Seth's window just looked like a black square.

"Seth says he can't hear me when it rains." And then she laughed. Kathy has a nice laugh, like Mama's.

At supper that same day, Mama and Daddy smiled at each other like they do when it's somebody's birthday.

"You and your mama are going on a field trip," Daddy said to us.

"Wow," said Kathy. "When?"

"Tomorrow," said Mama. "To the capital. We'll spend the whole day."

Kathy and I looked at each other and wiggled in our chairs. We like to study, but not so much that we don't like to get out of it once in a while. We made plans while we dried dishes.

We talked in our beds until we thought we heard Daddy coming down the hall.

It wasn't until we got on the bus with the other kids and mothers that I knew that Seth was going too.

I looked around Mama at Kathy, but she was already talking on her fingers just as nice as anything.

She pointed her first two fingers sideways and then flipped her little finger straight up. Seth and his mother sat in the seat behind Kathy. He leaned back in his seat and grinned at me. The bus started, and I looked out the window.

Seth is okay for a window friend, but he makes strange faces when he talks out loud. He sounds like he says *ar-lo* when he says hello to you.

"Here's how to spell HARRISBURG," said Kathy. She put her hand up by mine.

I watched her and then turned back to the window.

Sometimes when we passed a building, I could see my reflection beside me.

The capitol was even better than the pictures in Kathy's encyclopedia. It was all white and shiny by the river. It had a dome that was copper on the outside.

Inside, the dome was made of glass. Everywhere you looked there was some fine thing. The paintings on the walls were bigger than our bus, I think. And they all had gold frames, so wide and deep they looked like you could sit in them.

Some of the older boys tried to guess how high the dome was. Seth talked very loud. It sounded like when you try to talk underwater. The guide had to wait for him to stop so we could hear her.

I said to Kathy, "Why did Mrs. Abbott bring Seth?"

Kathy said, "I guess he wanted to see the capitol."

Seth stopped and looked at a painting like you look at something you have been wanting all your life and now you have it. Kathy tilted her head at him, and he spelled to her.

Kathy said, "He says he's going to paint a picture like this when we get home."

Mama laughed her laugh and patted his head.

"You do that," she said.

I held Mama's hand so I could keep walking and still look up at the inside of the dome. It seemed to turn over our heads, and when I looked straight ahead again, I felt a little dizzy.

We started up some marble steps. You could hear everyone's shoes. *Tap, clip, scuff.* There was an echo too.

Kathy said, "Listen to that. Everything sounds so big!" I wanted to listen, but just then Seth said something. He called to me, but I didn't look over.

We went into a room called the House of Representatives.

It was the shiniest, prettiest room I've ever seen. It had real gold on the walls. It had big gold lamps with hundreds of light bulbs, like Christmas trees hanging from the ceiling. There were lots of chairs with leather seats and desks that gleamed. Seth walked right under the ropes and sat in one of the chairs.

Mrs. Abbott got him to come back. He looked a little sad or something. He said, "On soun," which is what it sounds like when he says he's sorry.

Mrs. Abbott just smiled.

At the end we went to the gift shop. Kathy was trying on souvenir hats. Seth kept picking out hats too big for her.

They laughed so much that everyone in the store turned to look at them. I went around to the other side of the card rack.

I bought a pair of sunglasses that said HARRISBURG up where your eyebrows should be. Seth made so much noise about it that I took them off. He looked at me like he does when he doesn't understand what you are telling him.

And then he looked as if he did understand. He went away.

Now Seth was banging on the walls and screaming. "We'd better hurry," said the man. "Is there any way you can keep him from rocking the elevator?"

Mrs. Abbott just looked at the man, like she couldn't hear him.

I still had the sunglasses in my hand. They looked so big. I looked at the black square where Seth's yell was coming from. I wished we were all at home again, at the spelling window.

Then I had an idea, a spelling window idea. I went right over to the elevator and dropped my new sunglasses down the hole in the top.

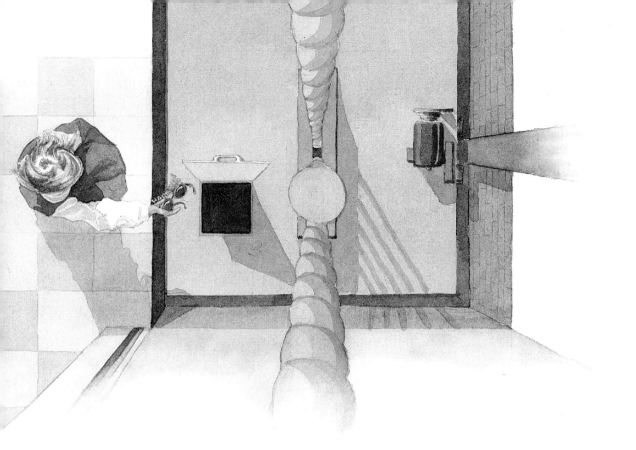

"Get back," said the guard.

"Shelly!" said Mama and Mrs. Abbott together.

Seth stopped screaming. Then we heard him laugh.

"Well, what do you know!" said the guard.

"Let's hustle," said the other men.

When the elevator finally came up and the doors swished open, there sat Seth with my sunglasses on his face.

He waved at us.

The next day, a man from the newspaper came and talked to me.

And the day after that, my picture was in the paper. I was standing with my arm around Seth's shoulders. He had my sunglasses on.

Now I am learning to spell at the spelling window. I still can't do as many words as Kathy.

But Seth says he'll teach me.

In the Silent World

Eileen M. Berry / illustrated by John Roberts

Have you ever imagined what it would be like to live in a silent world? Deaf people live each day in a

world that is nearly or completely silent. But that does not mean that their world is empty or boring.

Not all deaf people are born deaf. Some lose their hearing when they have a serious illness. Certain kinds of medicine can cause a hearing loss. Sometimes people lose all or part of their hearing when they listen to loud noises like music or machines over a long period of time. Older people often begin to lose their hearing as they age.

Being deaf does not make a person unable to live a normal life. People who have lost only part of their hearing can wear hearing aids. The most common hearing aids are small devices that fit in or behind the ear. Some hearing aids are so small that they cannot be seen from outside the ear. A larger kind of hearing aid is worn elsewhere on the body. Hearing

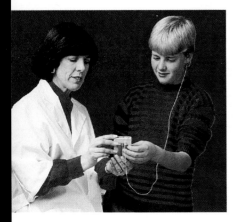

aids help some deaf people hear many of the sounds that hearing people do.

Some deaf people learn to speak. How do you think you would learn to speak if you had never heard the sounds of speech before? People can sometimes learn by watching other people's mouths making sounds and trying to copy them.

Many deaf people are able to understand the speech of people around them by watching the speaker's lips. A deaf person can have trouble *lip reading* if the speaker mumbles, shouts, turns his face sideways, or makes larger-than-normal mouth movements. Lip reading takes time and patience to learn. Even the best lip readers understand only about half of the words spoken to them. They guess the rest of the meaning by putting together the words they understood.

Sometimes deaf people use a special *sign language*. Each letter of the alphabet has a sign made with the fingers. Words and ideas also have signs made with one or both hands. Not only the hands but also the speaker's face and body can communicate his ideas. If the speaker has an exciting idea to talk about, he might lean forward and smile while signing. If he is

signing about something sad, he might frown and slump his shoulders.

Some deaf children attend special schools for the deaf. Sometimes the teachers at these schools use sign language to teach. Other deaf children go to public or private schools. They attend classes with hearing children, using a powerful hearing aid and sitting at the front of the classroom. Some public and private schools have separate classes for the deaf.

Deaf people can enjoy almost all of the things that hearing people can. They can "talk" on a special kind of telephone that lets them receive messages in print and then type their own message back. They can watch television programs by reading words printed at the bottom of the screen. They can buy alarm clocks, doorbells, and other devices that have flashing lights or vibrations in place of bells or buzzers. Some deaf people use hearing-ear dogs that are specially trained to alert them to important sounds.

Most deaf people have both deaf and hearing friends. Sometimes their hearing friends can talk with them in sign language, and sometimes they cannot. But anyone can learn the finger alphabet. If you are a hearing person, why not try to get to know a deaf friend better? Even if you don't know sign language, smiles and friendliness are two things that everyone understands.

Finger Alphabet

Alex,

the Drummer Boy

Steffi Adams
illustrated by Del Thompson and Chris Hartzler

This story is historical fiction. It takes place in January of 1781, when the colonies of America were fighting for their independence from England. The characters are real, and the story is based on a true event.

Patriot Spy

Alex McDonald's eyes sparkled as he stretched a piece of leather over his mother's clay water pot.

"I will m-m-make a drum fit for the g-g-great General Washington," he stuttered.

Alex put his homemade drum between his knees. He beat the drum with his hands, keeping time with the cold raindrops that fell all around the log cabin.

Alex imagined he felt the thick wool drummer's coat on his back. He could almost hear a musket ball whizzing through the crisp winter air.

"My drum would give orders to the soldiers," Alex thought. "We would drive the British from South Carolina. We would drive them toward General Washington."

Suddenly a hand touched his curly red hair. Alex jumped.

"Lad, I did not mean to frighten you," said Alex's father as he sat down on the porch. "I need your help."

Alex smiled. "I w-w-will do anything to help you, Father."

"I have heard that the British general, Cornwallis, will be leaving here soon," Mr. McDonald said. "He has ordered us to bring food to his camp. I want you to take our old bull and some taters. While the soldiers get the money for the food, you can look around the camp."

Alex's knees shook, and a hard lump settled in his stomach. "F-f-father, I c-c-cannot talk to s-s-strangers."

"You do not need to talk," said Mr. McDonald. "Just give them the food and keep your eyes and ears open. They will never guess that you are a patriot spy."

Mr. McDonald put his hand on his son's shoulder. "I have decided to join Daniel Morgan and the southern army," he said. "I need this information."

Alex looked into his father's kind face. "I will do my b-b-best," he promised.

Later that afternoon, the rain slowed down to a drizzle. Alex took the sack of potatoes and drove the old bull to the British camp. He gave the bull and the potatoes to a gruff British soldier. The soldier wore a red coat and carried a shiny musket.

"Are you a friend of the rebels or of the king?" asked the soldier.

"I-I-I . . . ," Alex stuttered. How could he answer such a question?

Another soldier laughed and slapped the guard's back. "You should not frighten children," he said to his friend. He turned to Alex. "Come with me. I will pay you for these supplies."

Alex and the British soldier splashed through a muddy lane between rows of small tents. Inside the tents, hungry, red-coated men shivered. Some of the men slept on layers of wet, dirty straw. Others played games or cleaned their muskets.

The British soldier stopped before a larger tent. "Wait here," he said. "I will bring your payment."

He returned and dropped some coins into Alex's hand. "Now off with you," he said kindly and went back inside the tent.

Alex walked slowly through the camp, listening to the soldiers call to each other. He looked up as a rider galloped into camp. The rider called to Alex, "Here, boy. Hold my horse."

Quickly, Alex stepped across a mud puddle and took the horse's reins. He watched the man enter General Cornwallis's large tent. He heard the man

say, "Sir, I have a letter from Lieutenant Colonel Tarleton."

Bloody Tarleton! Alex gasped. His father had told him about Colonel Tarleton. "The men call him 'Bloody' because he had our soldiers killed when they surrendered," Mr. McDonald had said. "He does not show mercy."

Alex leaned toward the tent flap. He heard about the British plans to destroy Daniel Morgan's army.

"I must warn Father," thought Alex. He handed the horse's reins to a passing soldier and walked away. At the edge of the camp, he began to run.

Patriot Messenger

The sun was just setting when Alex slammed the cabin door behind him. "F-F-Father," he gasped.

His father crossed the room and grabbed Alex's shoulders. "Slow down, lad, and tell me what is the matter."

Alex's mother stopped the hum of the spinning wheel, and his five sisters put down their sewing and knitting needles.

Alex took a deep breath. He told his father about the British plans.

Mr. McDonald hung a long knife from his belt. He picked up his rifle, his powder horn, and his black felt hat.

"Alex and I must reach General Morgan's camp before the rivers overflow," he told his wife. "Alex must tell the general all that he has seen and heard. We must warn him that the British are coming."

Mrs. McDonald nodded and turned toward the big stone fireplace. "I will pack some bread and meat," she said. "Alex, climb up into the loft. Put on your new mittens and stockings and get the thick quilt from your bed."

As he climbed into the loft, Alex wondered how he would ever answer General Morgan's questions.

The days passed as Alex and his father rode almost sixty miles through bare forests and rushing creeks. Cold wind and rain followed them all the way to General Morgan's camp in the northeast corner of South Carolina.

A guard dressed in a fringed leather hunting shirt led Alex and his father to Daniel Morgan's tent. "The general does not feel well," said the guard. "You must not stay too long."

Alex waited outside as his father stepped into the general's tent. A few minutes later, Mr. McDonald called Alex. Alex's heart pounded like a hammer as he entered the tent.

General Morgan groaned as he stood up and greeted Alex.

"The cold rains make my back and joints ache," explained the general. He pointed to a canvas folding chair. "Sit down, sir," he said to Mr. McDonald.

Mr. McDonald leaned his rifle against a tent pole and sat down. "This is my son, Alexander. He has some information for you."

Daniel Morgan stretched and looked at Alex. "Your father tells me you have been in the camp of that old fox Cornwallis. Is this true?"

Alex gulped and rubbed his sweaty palms against his shirt. "I-I-I w-w-went to . . . ," he began, but he could not finish. He hung his head in shame.

His father spoke quietly. "Alex stutters, sir."

The general lifted Alex up and set him on a rough wooden table.

"Twenty years ago I fought with the British against the French and the Indians. One day a musket ball went into the back of my neck and through my mouth. My wound healed, but it left behind this scar on my cheek," said Daniel Morgan. "For a long time I talked as if I had leather in my mouth. I had to speak slowly and carefully. You should do the same."

The general smiled at Alex. "Now try once more, my boy," he urged. "Tell me your story."

Alex took a deep breath and said, "Yes, sir. I took some taters and the old b-b-bull down to the British c-c-camp. Father told me not to f-f-forget anything I heard."

General Morgan opened a pouch which hung from his belt and pulled out a coin. "Tell me all you know," he said, handing the coin to Alex.

"No, thank you," Alex said, handing the coin back to the general. "I was near Lord C-C-Cornwallis's tent when a rider came into camp. The m-m-man was from Bloody Tarleton. He brought plans to d-d-destroy you. Lord C-C-Cornwallis ordered Colonel T-T-Tarleton to take a thousand men and fight you wherever you could be found. Lord C-C-Cornwallis will follow in a few days."

Once again General Morgan held out the gold coin. "My dear boy! You have given us information of great value. Now will you accept the gold piece?"

Alex shook his head.

"May I give you something else?" asked the general.

Alex blushed and said very softly, "I w-w-wish to be a drummer b-b-boy."

The general rubbed his chin. "When an officer gives a command, the drummer must beat out the proper signal," he said. "If a drummer gives the wrong signal, men could be killed or wounded. The battle could be lost."

"I would l-l-learn the signals," said Alex.

"Would you learn from the other drummers?" asked Daniel Morgan. "Would you obey the officers in all things?"

Alex looked into the general's eyes. "Yes, sir. I would do my b-b-best."

The general still was not sure. "My boy, the drummers are in great danger during each battle," he said. "The enemy will often shoot them because the drummers pass along the officers' orders to the men."

Alex jumped off the table. "Sir, I want to help d-d-drive the British from our land!"

"If your father agrees, you may stay," said General Morgan.

Mr. McDonald stared at the floor for what seemed like a long time. Finally, he raised his head and said, "You have a new drummer boy, General."

Drummer Boy

General Morgan introduced Alex to Jake Wilson, one of the older drummer boys. "Take care of him, Jake," said the general before he left. "Show him all the drum signals that he must know."

Jake smiled and handed Alex his drum. "This is our special practice time," he said to Alex. "The soldiers know that all the drummers are practicing their signals. They will ignore us."

"May I practice by m-m-myself?" asked Alex.

Jake shook his head. "No, you must never beat the drum for fun. The soldiers would think that you were giving them a signal. Now, listen well," Jake added, "this is your first signal."

Alex listened carefully to each signal. He learned to strike his drum with steady strokes.

The days passed. Alex learned to beat short strokes, long strokes, and quick drumrolls.

One week later, on January 16, Alex and Jake shivered as they marched beside the soldiers in blue coats. Alex and Jake carried red drums the color of Alex's heavy coat.

Alex listened carefully. His friend Jake was beating his drum. Jake's drum said, "Front to halt!" Alex passed the signal to the other drummers, and the whole army stopped.

General Morgan pointed toward Cowpens, where thousands of cattle grazed each spring.

"We'll stand and fight here," he said. "On this ground I will defeat the British or lay my bones."

Alex and the other drummers beat the camp
signal. Some of the soldiers gathered wood, made
campfires, and dried their wet clothes. Some passed
out food and gunpowder from the wagons. Others
fed and watered their horses. The scouts guarded
the camp.

After supper, Alex visited his father's campfire.
"Will we h-h-have enough men to f-f-fight?" he asked.

"Riflemen are coming from miles around," said
Alex's father as he cleaned his rifle. "We will give
Bloody Tarleton a good fight."

The night passed slowly. Daniel Morgan walked from campfire to campfire. He joked with the men and explained his battle plan.

"Keep in good spirits and the day will be ours," he said.

Later that night, Alex saw the general limp into the nearby woods. He nudged Jake. "Where is the general going?" he whispered.

Jake rolled over. "General Morgan always prays for our protection during a battle," he said. "Go to sleep."

Alex felt much safer. He was sure that God would protect their army.

Early the next morning, the scouts rode into camp. "Tarleton is only five miles away!" they shouted.

General Morgan yelled, "Boys, get up!"

Alex ran to his drum. He hung it around his neck. Then he and the other drummers beat the signals on their drums.

"Prepare to march!"

"Form companies!"

The soldiers and riflemen quickly threw their belongings into the wagons. As the men lined up, the wagons jolted into the woods behind the field.

Alex and the other drummers gave the marching signal. The men marched onto the grassy, sloping field. They formed three long battle lines.

General Morgan rode along the two front lines.

"Wait until the enemy is close," he said. "Fire two shots and then retreat to the second line."

Alex's father waited in the second line. He lay in the high grass with the rest of the riflemen.

The soldiers in Alex's company stood in the third line, near the top of the grassy slope.

"I have confidence in your skill and courage," said General Morgan to the men in Alex's company. "Stand firm and obey your officer, Colonel Howard. Soldiers on horses are waiting behind the hill to surprise the British."

Alex watched as one thousand British soldiers lined up behind two cannons. He saw British horsemen in green uniforms and soldiers in bright red coats. He also saw Scottish soldiers who wore kilts and played bagpipes.

While Alex watched, fifty British horsemen galloped toward the front line. Morgan's riflemen fired, and black smoke covered the field. When the smoke cleared, fifteen of the horsemen had fallen from their saddles. The others were riding back to the trees.

The riflemen turned and ran to the second line. Behind them, cannons roared, and the British soldiers marched forward.

Alex saw his father in the second line. He watched his father take aim and retreat up the slope.

Suddenly Alex gasped. His father had fallen! "Father, get up!" Alex yelled.

"Drummer, order the men to fire!" shouted Colonel Howard.

A Promise Kept

Alex wanted to run to his father, but he had promised to obey the officers. For thirty minutes, Alex beat his drum, trying not to look at the place where his father lay.

"Make ready!" "Fire!" "Cease firing!"

"Make ready!" "Fire!" "Cease firing!"

Again and again, Alex beat his drum until his arms were so tired that they felt as wooden as his drumsticks.

Alex looked up as Colonel Howard stopped beside him. "Tell your men to turn and face the soldiers on their right side," the colonel said.

Again Alex lifted his drumsticks. There was no time to think. He quickly beat the signal.

"We must win," he thought. "We must win!"

Alex watched as the men in his company turned and retreated. Soon the whole line was retreating.

"I gave the wrong s-s-signal," Alex cried.

General Morgan rode over to Alex and Colonel Howard. "Why are your men retreating?" he asked. "Are they beaten?"

"Do men who march like that look like they are beaten?" asked Colonel Howard.

General Morgan watched the men and quickly decided on a new plan. "I will tell them when to face about and fire," he said to Colonel Howard.

Alex looked down the long line. Where was Jake? "I cannot g-g-give the signal," he said to the men.

"Jake has been wounded," General Morgan said. "I am depending on you."

Alex had no choice. "Dear God, please h-h-help me," he prayed.

When the soldiers had reached a certain spot,
General Morgan said to Alex, "Beat the signal to face
about! Give them one fire, and the day is ours!"

Quickly Alex beat three single strokes, then a short
and a long stroke. He watched as the soldiers turned,
knelt, and fired.

At the same moment, American horsemen and
riflemen surrounded the British. Colonel Tarleton
and two hundred British horsemen broke through
the lines and galloped away. Many of the British
soldiers threw down their guns, knelt, and begged
for mercy.

Alex ran down the hill past fallen men. He knelt by
his father. "Father, are y-y-you all right?" he asked.

Mr. McDonald raised his head. "A musket ball hit
my leg," he said. "Would you go to the wagons and
get my horse? I will ride back to camp and get my leg
bandaged."

General Morgan stopped beside them. "I'll give
Alex a ride back to the camp, Mr. McDonald. Then he
can bring your horse back."

He held out his hand to Alex. "We have won the
day, drummer boy!"

One of a Kind

Milly Howard

illustrated by Keith Neely

Bits and Pieces

"Made it!" Roger yelled as the soccer ball sailed past his friend Pete. "Five goals in a row!" he said, as Pete ran for the ball. "Let's see you beat that!"

Roger's dad turned into the driveway. He stopped the station wagon and got out. The ball sailed across the yard. "Good kick, Pete!" he called. "You boys are getting pretty good!"

"Thanks, Mr. Cord." Pete grinned and followed Roger to the car.

Roger peered into the big box. "What's that, Dad?"

"Oh, just bits and pieces from different bikes. I know a boy who needs a new bike. I thought I could put one together for him. You boys want to help?"

"Sure," the boys replied.

"How about carrying the box into the garage while I change into my work clothes?" asked Mr. Cord.

He opened the back door and went inside. The boys tugged the box into the garage and began to look at the bike parts.

"Boy, your dad was right when he said they were from different bikes," said Pete. He held up a scratched fender. "This one is red, and the other one is blue. Why would he want to go to all the trouble to put a bike together for someone else?"

"Dad is always doing things for other people," replied Roger. "He goes with the pastor to visit people in town. When he meets someone who needs something, he tries to help."

"But why would he go to all the work of putting a bike together when he could just buy one?"

"Bikes aren't all that cheap," Roger replied. "I should know. I've been saving for a new one for almost a year."

Pete put the fender back into the box and looked up. "What kind do you want?" he asked.

Roger's eyes sparkled. "A Silver Streak," he replied.

"Wow!" said Pete. "The Silver Streak is the best! How much money do you have?"

Roger sighed. "Not very much. I get an allowance, but I'm supposed to buy my school supplies out of that. It doesn't go very far."

The door slammed behind Mr. Cord. "Ready, boys?"

134

Mr. Cord took some pieces of sandpaper out of a box. "Why don't you sand the paint off the fenders?"

Roger pulled out a blue fender, and Pete picked up a red one.

135

An hour later Pete stretched and put down his tattered sandpaper. "I've got to go home," he said. "If I don't, I'll be late for supper."

"Thanks for the help, Pete," said Mr. Cord.

"See you later, Pete," said Roger. He walked with Pete to the garage door and then came back to look at the bike frame his dad was putting together. "Think it's going to work, Dad?" he asked.

"Mm-hmm," Mr. Cord replied. "I think I have enough parts." He stood up and wiped his hands. "Time for us to stop too."

Roger helped him put away the tools and clean up the garage before they went inside to eat.

The next afternoon Roger and Pete raced home from school on their bikes.

"Beat you!" Pete called, braking at the Cords' house.

Roger's wheels spun as he turned into the driveway. "Just wait," he said, frowning. "When I get my Silver Streak, you won't stand a chance."

Pete just laughed. "Want to come over to my house?"

Roger glanced at the garage. The bike frame lay propped against the workbench.

"No, " he said slowly, "I have to do my homework and then help Dad work on the bike when he gets home."

"Why? It's not your bike," Pete said.

"Dad wants me to help," Roger replied.

"Every day? Glad it's you and not me," called Pete as he pedaled away. "See you tomorrow."

When Mr. Cord got home, Roger was already in the garage, sanding the frame.

"Hi, Dad," he said, looking up.

His father grinned. "I'm glad to see you working already, Roger." He ran his hand lightly over the frame. "What do you think of it?"

Roger shook his head. "Well, it's no Silver Streak," he said. "But I guess if you didn't have a bike . . . ," his voice trailed off.

"Just be patient. You might be surprised. I'll change my clothes and be right out."

Do It Right

By supper time the frame of the bike was almost free of paint. Roger put down the sandpaper and stretched. "I'm starving," he said.

Mr. Cord nodded. "You've done a good job, Roger," he said. "This may take less time than I thought."

Tired as he was, Roger enjoyed hearing his father's praise. He helped put the tools away and then went inside the house. "Dad," he asked, "do I know the boy?"

"What boy?" His father reached for an old cloth and soap to wash his hands.

"The boy who gets the bike," Roger replied.

"Oh, that boy." Mr. Cord smiled at Roger. "Just wait and see."

Roger gave him a puzzled look, but Mr. Cord just smiled again and tossed a towel to Roger. "I thought you were starving," he said.

Roger wiped his hands hastily. "I sure am! Let's go!"

The next week Roger and Mr. Cord spent most of their afternoons in the garage. Mr. Cord worked slowly, taking care that each part was in good shape and fit perfectly.

"Why are you being so picky?" Roger asked when Mr. Cord rejected a part that looked fine to Roger.

"Son, if you want to do something . . ."

Roger grinned and finished, " . . . do it right."

Mr. Cord laughed. "Do I say that a lot?"

He wiped his hands as Roger nodded. "Well, this is for a special boy," Mr. Cord added.

"Special?" Roger looked up quickly with interest. "Still not going to tell me?"

"Nope." Mr. Cord reached into his pocket for his keys. "Why don't you clean these parts while I run down to the hardware store and pick up what I need."

As Mr. Cord left, Pete rode up on his bike. "Hi, Roger. Still working?" he asked.

Roger stretched. "It's taking a long time to fix this bike. Where are you going?"

"Soccer practice," Pete replied. "You're not going?"

Roger clapped his hand to his head. "I forgot!"

"Well, hurry up," Pete said. "We're going to be late."

Roger shook his head. "I can't. I told Dad I would clean these parts."

"Tell your mother you have to go to practice. She'll tell your dad when he comes back." Pete turned his bike around.

Roger hesitated. He hadn't played all week. He shook his head. "No, I'll wait until Dad comes back."

Pete gave a disgusted shake of his head. Roger stood still and watched him pedal back up the street. Then he turned slowly back to work.

"This dumb bike," he grumbled to himself. "I wouldn't be surprised if it falls apart when that boy tries to ride it!"

Roger began to rub the metal. When his father came back, the parts were almost clean. Intent on his work, Roger had forgotten about soccer. He and his father worked for another hour or so. Then Roger stood back to look.

"Hey, Dad," he said in surprise. "It's starting to look like a real bike!"

Mr. Cord just grinned and picked up his tools. Roger helped, stopping from time to time to look at the bike thoughtfully.

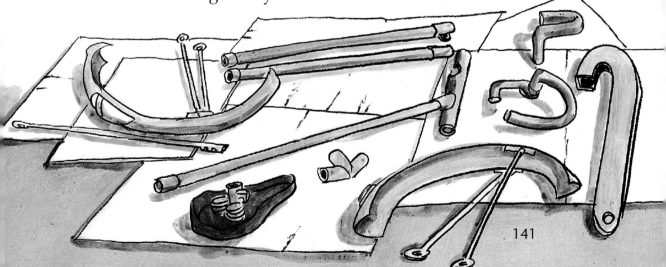

141

"You know something, Dad," he said as they closed the garage doors. "That bike would look good painted blue."

Mr. Cord nodded. "That's exactly what I was thinking," he said. "I picked up some blue paint at the hardware store. And some silver too."

"What's the silver for?" Roger asked.

"Oh, I thought you might want to decorate the bike some way," Mr. Cord said. "I'll leave that up to you."

After supper Roger went upstairs to look through his books. He couldn't find what he wanted. Even the Silver Streak wasn't quite right. Finally, he picked up a paper and pencil and began to draw.

Lightning

The next afternoon Mr. Cord found Roger in the garage, paper and pencil in hand.

"Look at this, Dad." Roger handed him the paper.

"This is good, Roger," Mr. Cord said slowly, looking from the paper to the bike. "And I think we can do it too! We'll have to be careful, though, to get it just right. After I spray the bike blue, you can paint the decorations yourself."

"Really?" Roger was delighted. "Thanks, Dad!"

He watched as Mr. Cord sprayed the bike frame. "How long will it take to put the rest of it together?" he asked eagerly.

"Not too long," his father replied. "Everything is ready. When this is dry, you can decorate it, and we'll put it together."

The next afternoon Roger raced home and charged upstairs to change his clothes. "I'll be out in the garage, Mom," he called and ran out again.

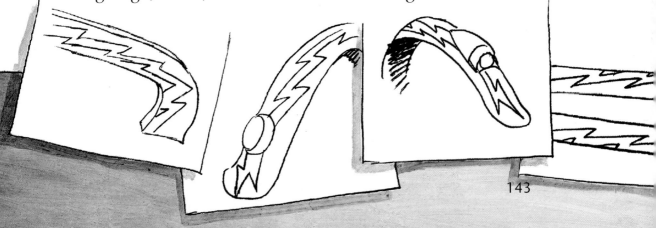

When Mr. Cord turned into the driveway, the bike frame was already painted. Silver handlebars glinted in the afternoon sunlight, silver racing stripes sparkled, and down the back fender a streak of silver lightning flashed against dark blue.

"It looks great, Roger!" Mr. Cord leaned forward to inspect the paint. "Is it dry?"

"Yes, sir," Roger replied. "Can we put it together?"

"Sure thing. I'll be back in a minute."

When Mr. Cord came back outside, Mrs. Cord was with him. She stopped beside Roger and watched as Mr. Cord put the last parts on the bike. Then Mr. Cord stood up and steadied the bike on its kickstand.

"You two did a great job," Mrs. Cord said, smiling. "That's the best bike I've ever seen."

"Well, it's one of a kind," Mr. Cord said. "But I think it needs a name, don't you, Roger?"

"Sir?" Roger took his eyes off the bike and looked at his father. "Oh, yes, sir. It has one—'Lightning.' "

His mother and father looked at each other as Roger turned back to the bike. "Lightning? That sounds good to me," said Mr. Cord. "Well, we're going in. Are you coming?"

"In a minute," Roger replied.

After they were gone, Roger walked around the bike. "One of a kind," he said to himself. "I wish . . ."

The next morning he was awakened by his father shaking his shoulder. "Wake up, Son. It's Saturday. Time to deliver the bike!"

Roger groaned. "The boy!"

All through breakfast he felt a little sick. "I'm being selfish," he thought to himself. "Wanting a bike that Dad made for someone else!"

His feet seemed to drag as he followed his father to the garage. Lightning stood on its kickstand where it had been left. Mr. Cord wheeled it out of the driveway. The early-morning sunlight picked out the silver sparkles.

146

"Well, Son, what do you think?" Mr. Cord asked.

"It's a great bike, Dad." Roger swallowed hard.

"As good as the Silver Streak?" Mr. Cord asked.

Roger tried to smile. "Better, Dad. This bike is one of a kind, remember? Where are we going to deliver it?"

"It's already been delivered," Mr. Cord said. "It's yours."

Roger stared. "Mine! But why didn't you say so?"

"Would you have wanted it at first?" Mr. Cord asked.

Roger shook his head, remembering how he had wanted a Silver Streak.

"We just couldn't afford a Silver Streak, Roger," Mr. Cord said. "I hope this one will do."

"It will, Dad. It will!" Roger gave his father a hug.

Pete rode by, waved, and then stopped to look again. Roger looked at his father.

Mr. Cord chuckled. "Go ahead, Son."

Roger hopped on the bike and spun out of the driveway. Wild whoops split the Saturday morning quiet as the two bikes raced down the street.

Jim

Gwendolyn Brooks
illustrated by Mary Ann Lumm

There never was a nicer boy
Than Mrs. Jackson's Jim.
The sun should drop its greatest gold
On him.

Because, when Mother-dear was sick,
He brought her cocoa in.
And brought her broth, and brought her bread,
And brought her medicine.

And, tipping, tidied up her room.
And would not let her see
He missed his game of baseball
Terribly.

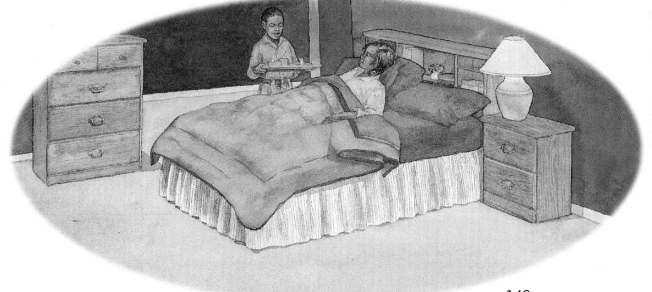

149

Pecos Bill

(a tall tale)

Becky
Davis

illustrated
by
Bruce Day

A tale is a story that someone has invented to make folks laugh or cry or think. Some tales, at least the especially good ones, do more than that. They make you slap your knee and guffaw or roll on the floor and howl. Those stories are tall tales. They are the tales that just can't be true, but sure as a shooting star you wish they really could come true.

Pecos Looks for a Horse

Away out West where the coyotes howl, there lived the rootinest, tootinest cowboy of all. His name was Pecos Bill.

Now Pecos Bill wasn't like just any cowboy that you see every day. Some said that he had grown up on the desert with a pack of coyotes. And sometimes the other cowboys almost believed the old tale. Why, Pecos could outhowl the biggest wolf, outfight the meanest grizzly bear, and outrun the fastest horse.

Before any other cowboy could get his foot in the stirrup, Pecos had run almost into the next county. But still, the cowboys thought that Pecos looked strange running around the range on foot.

150

"Bill," said Gun Smith, "no self-respecting cowboy should be seen running around the range without a horse. It just doesn't seem right."

Pecos scratched his neck with a spiny cactus leaf. "You know, Smith," he replied, "maybe you are right. Maybe I should get a horse. But one thing is certain. I will not ride one of those poky horses you keep in your corrals. I must find one that is as swift as lightning and as terrifying as thunder."

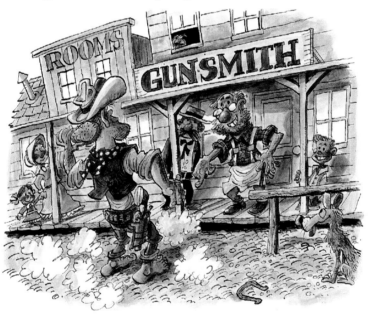

And without so much as a by-your-leave or a wish-me-well, Pecos Bill vanished over the hillside. Gun Smith stood in Pecos's dust, scratching his head and wondering again how Bill ever learned to run so fast. Maybe the coyotes really had taught him!

Pecos Bill ran on into the next state. In every town he stopped to ask if anyone had heard of a horse that was faster than a lightning bolt.

"Well, sir," drawled one old rancher, "I've heard tell of a big horse that runs so fast that no one can tell if he's white or gold."

The other townsfolk shook their heads. "You'll never catch that horse, though," they warned. "He's never been roped and never been ridden."

Pecos just laughed. But in every town he heard the same story.

"They call him Widow Maker," said the barber, leaning over to shave Pecos's chin. "Any man who wants to ride Widow Maker might as well tell his family good-bye!"

Pecos chuckled as he rubbed his chin. "Widow Maker?" he said and laughed outright.

He thanked the barber and raced away. In the next two days he ran from the plains of Montana to the border of Mexico. He ran until his feet ached from running. But never, never did he catch sight of Widow Maker.

Well, Pecos Bill finally gave up looking for that horse. He tried riding just about everything else he could think of.

He saddled a lightning bolt and rode it. It was fast enough, but it went only one direction—down!

He saddled a tornado and rode it across the plains. It twisted this way and that. When Pecos got off, his head was spinning around and around.

"No, nothing will do except a horse," he said to himself. Pecos sat down under a cactus to rest. He watched an ant crawl into a hole in the sand, then struggle up the other side.

"That looks like a hoofprint," Pecos said sleepily. "But it can't be. I've never seen a hoofprint as big as a dinner plate."

Then he sat up and looked again. "As big as a dinner plate!" His shout echoed in the canyon. "That must have been made by Widow Maker!"

Widow Maker

Pecos jumped up and ran, following the trail
Widow Maker had left. From time to time the prints
joined smaller hoofprints.

"There must be nine hundred eighty-seven mares
in this herd," Pecos thought. "And Widow Maker
looks like the leader."

After a few days, he saw the horses grazing at the
bottom of a canyon. The nine hundred eighty-seven
mares tossed their manes and whinnied. But Pecos
had no time for them. He watched the big mustang
standing in the middle of the herd. Widow Maker
was twice as tall as the mares. He was golden all
over except for a white mane, a white tail, and
white legs.

"That is the horse I will have," Pecos declared. He
tied his rope into a lariat and lassoed Widow Maker.

With one snort and a powerful jump, Widow Maker
raced away. The rope snapped like a banjo string.

Pecos Bill grinned. "That horse has spirit," he said.
"But so have I!"

And off Pecos raced after Widow Maker. All that
afternoon, all that night, and all the next day Pecos
raced the mustang. Widow Maker tossed his mane

and whinnied, almost as if he were laughing at the man who dared to try to catch him.

But Pecos did not give up. On the third day of the long chase, Widow Maker jumped over a little mountain and caught his hoof on a rock. It was only a split second before he was up and running again. But that split second was all Pecos Bill needed. With one leap, he landed on Widow Maker's back.

"Ya-hoo!" Pecos yelled.

Widow Maker kicked hard enough to send any other man to the top of Pike's Peak. But Pecos hung on tighter.

Widow Maker reared up so high that any other man would have hit the ground hard enough to make another Grand Canyon in the West. But Pecos just hung on tighter.

Widow Maker flipped a double flip and rolled over in the dirt so many times that any other man would have been crushed flat. But Pecos Bill hung on.

At last Widow Maker stood panting with his head hung low, as if to say, "You win, cowboy. I've met my match."

Pecos patted Widow Maker on the neck. "Widow Maker," he said, "you're the only creature I've ever met that gave me a good fight. I admire you for that. So I'm going to give you a choice."

Pecos got off Widow Maker's back and sat down on a rock. He broke open a cactus for himself and one for Widow Maker. They both drank thirstily. "You see, Widow Maker," Pecos said, "we have a big job to do. This wild West has to be tamed. I might be able to do it all by myself, but it would take me a long time. You can help me do it faster."

Widow Maker tossed his mane and stomped his hoof.

"Now, you could go back to your free and easy life," said Pecos Bill. "Or you could help me finish this big job. It's up to you."

Widow Maker trotted back and forth. Pecos Bill waited, not saying anything else. After a while,

Widow Maker trotted back up to Pecos. He pushed his muzzle into Pecos Bill's hand.

The cowboys stared in amazement that evening as they saw who rode into camp. Pecos Bill and Widow Maker! What a team!

From that time on, Pecos Bill and Widow Maker set out to tame the West. And tame it they did—from the Mississippi River to the California coast. But Widow Maker never let anyone ride him except Pecos Bill. Anyone else who tried took a quick trip to Pike's Peak.

And, believe me, it's a long walk home from Pike's Peak!

David Livingstone:
Man of Determination

Jan Joss

illustrated by
Del Thompson
and Sam
Laterza

One of the first white men to explore the interior of Africa was a Scottish missionary doctor. He wanted to open up Africa to missions. During his explorations, David Livingstone preached the gospel to many.

A Book I Can Study

David Livingstone quietly ate his bread and cheese, wishing he were going to school instead of to work. Beginning today, he would get to study only late at night, after work.

"You need to hurry a little, David," his mother whispered. "You don't want to be late for work your first day."

All around them his younger brothers and sisters still slept. No matter how hard his father worked as a tea merchant, there was not enough money for the big family to live on. So David, at ten, had a job. The money that David could earn would help to buy food.

David arrived at the cotton factory. He found that he was to walk a row of spinning spools. He was to watch the big frames for thinning threads and piece them  before they broke. Back and forth he walked across the spinning jenny, from before dawn to eight at night.

David worked six days. By Saturday his feet were sore from climbing over and under the spinning frame, and his head throbbed from the clattering machines. But when he received his first pay, David was happy. Mother stood quietly as he handed her the money. Tears glistened in her eyes. She placed some of the money back in David's hand.

"David, you keep part of this. Buy what you wish," she said.

David hurried to the bookstore. The storekeeper was dimming the lamps to close, but he waited while David searched for the book he wanted and brought it to the counter.

The old man looked at David over his glasses. "Are you sure that is the book you want?"

"Oh, yes, sir," David answered.

"Can you read Latin?" the man asked.

"No, sir," said David.

The storekeeper looked puzzled. "Why not get a book you can read?"

"That would be too easy. I want a book I can study," said David.

At first the book seemed almost too hard. But in his spare time, David studied hard. He was determined to learn Latin.

The other children at work did not understand David. He often took a book to work and balanced it on the spinning jenny. Each time he passed the book, he read a minute until it was time to continue his walk along the frames. Sometimes the boys tried to knock his book down by throwing thread bobbins at it. When they did, David just put the book back up and kept on studying.

Every night David left the factory tired. But every night he continued his studies.

"I hope I can finish this science book tonight," David thought as he walked home in the moonlight.

Mother met him at the door. The one-room apartment was silent; the other children were asleep in their beds on the floor. David ate his porridge and quietly studied by the light from the lamp.

Around midnight David's mother awoke. "It's late, David. Morning will come quickly."

David hadn't quite finished the book, but he put out the lamp and climbed wearily into his bed.

David received some training at home and at Sabbath school as well. His father was a Sabbath-school teacher and a member of a missionary society. David's father encouraged him to memorize long Bible passages.

David began to like science very much. When he had a little spare time, he collected herbs and rocks. As time went on, his books began to make him feel that the Bible and science did not agree. He questioned the things his father had taught him.

When he was a young man, David read a book that helped him to see that the Bible and true science do not go against each other. And when he understood that fact he accepted Christ's salvation for himself.

The Smoke of a Thousand Villages

"You'll never have enough money to go to the university; give up!" Many men in the factory laughed at David.

"I'll not give up studying. Someday I will go to the university," David always answered. He knew that the Lord wanted him to become a missionary doctor. But to be a doctor, he would have to go to college.

David worked and saved for years and finally had enough money to start at the university. First he would learn to preach; then he would become a doctor.

One day he heard a preacher who had worked in Africa. "Africa needs the Word of God," Mr. Moffat said. "I have seen the smoke of a thousand villages, villages where no white man has ever gone!"

"I will go there," David said in his heart. "I will take God's message to the people of Africa."

Dr. David Livingstone finally finished his training. The Livingstone family had one final evening together before he was to leave.

"We should stay up and talk all night," Dr. Livingstone told his family.

Of course his mother didn't agree to that. "No, David, you need your rest to travel."

"We'll get up early and read the Bible together," his father said.

At five o'clock the next morning, the family gathered to read the Scripture. " 'The Lord shall preserve thee from all evil; He shall preserve thy soul,' " Dr. Livingstone read.

His father led in prayer. Then, in turn, the other family members prayed for David. As they later said good-bye to him, they wondered whether they would ever see him again.

On November 17, 1840, David Livingstone left his home in England to serve the Lord in Africa.

Dr. Livingstone arrived at the mission station, the home of Mr. Moffat and his family. Livingstone's first task was to learn a new language. So he moved away from the mission to learn the ways and language of the nationals.

Then Livingstone set out to visit tribes that had never heard of God. Many listened to him tell about God. They listened to the hymns he sang. They were fascinated by the "magic lantern" slide pictures that he showed. Yet only God could reach their hearts.

One tribe that Dr. Livingstone tried to reach had an unusual problem. Many lions had been destroying their sheep, cattle, goats, and sometimes even people.

"Why don't you kill the lions?" Dr. Livingstone asked the people.

"The lions have evil spirits in them," a man answered.

The doctor shook his head. "These lions are like any others," he said. "They don't have evil spirits. If we kill one great lion, the others may flee to another valley."

A messenger came running to David. "Lions are attacking our sheep," he called.

David grabbed his gun and ran with the messenger to the village. He shouted to the frightened villagers to kill the lion. But the villagers fell back, shaking their heads. Livingstone fired both barrels of his gun at the lion.

The lion seemed unhurt.

Livingstone began to reload his gun. The lion turned and leaped. Its big jaws came together on Livingstone's shoulder.

Livingstone's friend fired. Then the fierce lion turned on him.

Another man rushed to help. He too was hurt by the lion.

At last the wounded lion fell. The battle was over, but three men had been badly hurt. Dr. Livingstone had to give instructions to others who set his injured arm.

Another chief sent a messenger to Dr. Livingstone inviting the doctor to visit his tribe. When Dr. Livingstone arrived, he found some women crying beside a hut. "The chief's only son is sick," one woman told him.

Dr. Livingstone knew that his medicine might help the boy. But if the medicine failed, the people would

be very angry. Then they might not want to hear about God.

"Lord," Dr. Livingstone prayed, "show me what to do."

God gave Dr. Livingstone courage to try his medicine on the boy.

The next morning the chief's son was able to sit up and eat. He had begun to get well.

"Why do you come?" the chief asked. "I have heard of white men who come to our coast for ivory or slaves."

"I came to tell you about God, who loves you," Dr. Livingstone replied.

Up River

The next year Dr. Livingstone married Mary Moffat, who had grown up on her father's mission station. For several years David and Mary worked together, teaching and training many people and raising a family.

Dr. Livingstone was concerned for the people in the north. He also knew that Africa needed a mission to train the nationals. He was determined to find a place in the north to build that mission. After making several exploration trips with his family, Dr. Livingstone learned that there was danger in the jungle far worse than lions—fever. Often his wife and children became ill. If Dr. Livingstone had not known medicine himself, they could not have survived.

During the years of river exploration, Dr. Livingstone's wife became ill again and returned to Scotland. Later she finally got back to Africa, but she had been with Livingstone only a short time when she died.

Dr. Livingstone was still determined. He made a trip back to England to visit his children and to raise more funds. Then he returned to Africa with a new idea. He was sure that if he could find the headwaters of the big Nile River, he would open up a passage into Africa so that Christian missionaries could get in.

This time Livingstone selected a party of all nationals and started out on foot. Again he preached and kept journals. Two big problems made Dr. Livingstone's work hard. Arab slave dealers were causing great trouble for the nationals, and many of Livingstone's helpers ran away.

One group of nationals ran away and got safely back to the coast. Since they didn't want to get in trouble for deserting the exploring party, they told lies.

"He is dead," the nationals told Dr. Livingstone's friends.

"We were attacked by savages," one said.

"I hid in the bushes and saw it all," another said.

In England, news headlines announced, "David Livingstone is dead." Some did not believe the story. Others felt that Dr. Livingstone's body should be found and brought back to England.

An American newspaper sent an Englishman named Henry Stanley to lead a search. This brave man looked for Livingstone for a long time. When Stanley finally found Livingstone, Arab slave dealers had stolen all of Livingstone's supplies. He was sick and needed help very badly. The two men camped together for several months. Dr. Livingstone was grateful to have Mr. Stanley's company. It had been six years since he had seen an Englishman.

Stanley's good food and medical supplies brought Livingstone back to better health.

Stanley wrote of Livingstone in his journal:

His gentleness never forsakes him, his hopefulness never deserts him.

Stanley was not able to talk Dr. Livingstone into returning to England with him.

Livingstone kept trying to find the headwaters of the Nile. He became ill again and was cared for by his friends. But this time Dr. Livingstone could not get well. He died in the Africa he loved.

Dr. Livingstone never found the headwaters of the Nile, but his exploring and writings made it possible for other missionaries to get into Africa with the riches of the gospel.

Esther, the Queen

(based on the Book of Esther)

Becky Davis

illustrated by Del Thompson and John Roberts

After the days of King Solomon, God's people became more and more disobedient. The judgment of God brought mighty nations to capture Israel and to carry away many people to foreign lands. Even though God allowed His people to be punished, He was watchful and protected them. The following account adapted from the Book of Esther clearly shows God's protecting hand on His people, the Jews.

The King's House

Esther was just finishing her weaving when Mordecai came running in with the latest news from the palace.

"I have heard," he said, "that the queen has made King Ahasuerus angry. The stories say that he will be sending her away."

Esther gasped. "Send away Queen Vashti? But who will be our queen?"

"There are rumors . . . but I do not know if they are true." Mordecai hesitated. "The rumors say that he will be looking for a new wife among the beautiful young girls of his lands."

177

The stories Mordecai had heard were true. Announcements were posted the next day. The officers came to all the homes in all the far corners of King Ahasuerus's lands. They took lovely girls back to the palace. Esther was among them. She thanked God that Mordecai lived near the palace. There was still a chance that she might see him sometimes.

Esther remembered what Mordecai had told her. "Do not tell anyone that you are a Jewess," he had said. "And do not tell anyone that you are my cousin." Esther obeyed him and breathed not a word of her background.

Hegai was in charge of all the women. There were princesses who had been brought from far away. There were humble shepherdesses and village girls whose eyes were dazzled by the beauty and splendor of the palace. What noise and confusion there was!

As time passed, Hegai took the beautiful maidens one by one to see the king. Hegai gave the maidens any lovely garment, jewelry, or scent they wanted to help them be their best.

Some of the maidens selfishly demanded the best of everything. They took hours to become as beautiful as they could be. But when Esther's time came, she smiled at Hegai. "You know much better than I what would please the king," she said honestly. "I will wear what you choose to give me."

Hegai was pleased. "Esther is a sensible girl," he thought.

Hegai spent more time carefully arranging her clothes and fixing her hair than he had spent on any of the other women. When he had finished, even the other women had to admit that Esther was beautiful.

"I'm sure that you will please the king, Esther," Hegai said.

Esther did not regret letting Hegai choose her apparel. The king chose her over all the other women to be his queen.

But Esther still didn't tell anyone that she was a Jewess.

Mordecai was serving at the palace gate. Sometimes he heard people whispering. One day someone whispered to him, "Two servants are plotting to kill the king!"

"I must tell Esther about this," thought Mordecai. "She can take a message to the king."

Quickly Mordecai wrote a note and gave it to a messenger. "Deliver this to your queen immediately," he instructed.

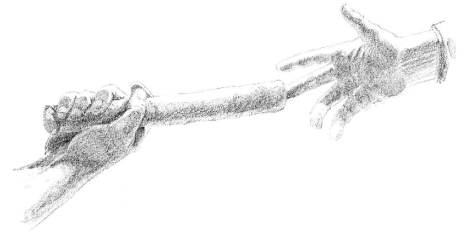

When Esther read the letter, she realized that King Ahasuerus was in great danger. When the king sent for her, Esther showed him Mordecai's message.

"What is this? Servants are plotting to kill me?" Ahasuerus roared in his rage. "I am the most powerful king on earth, and they plot to kill me?"

Quickly King Ahasuerus sent spies to investigate the plot to kill him. They found out that what the man Mordecai had said was true.

"Hang both of the men," King Ahasuerus ordered. "We will show how dangerous it is to plot to kill a king."

Turning to his scribe, he said, "Write of this matter in the chronicles of the king."

Then Ahasuerus took Esther's hand. "You honor your king," he said. "You have helped to save my life."

Haman's Plot

In the kingdom there lived a prince named Haman. Haman knew just how to please King Ahasuerus. The king promoted him to be chief of all the princes. Now only the king himself was more important than Haman.

Haman liked to see all the servants bowing down to him. "I am a very important man," he thought. "Everyone honors me."

But Esther's cousin, Mordecai, would not bow down to Haman. The other servants whispered, "Mordecai, that is Haman! The king has commanded that we bow to him. Why do you not do it?"

Mordecai replied, "I am a Jew. I worship only the one true God."

Day after day Mordecai refused to bow. The other servants didn't understand why he wouldn't bow with them. Finally, they told Haman about Mordecai.

The next day when Haman marched through the gate, he searched the crowds of people. There, off to the side, he saw Mordecai. Mordecai did not bow or even stand up.

"What are you doing?" Haman shouted. "Do you not know that I am Haman, the chief of all the princes?"

Mordecai just looked at him and answered quietly. "I am a Jew. I worship only the one true God."

Haman turned pale with anger and stalked away.

"I will kill Mordecai," he thought. "And I will kill all the other Jews too. Then there will not be anyone who will refuse to bow down to me."

The next day Haman went before the king. "There is a people in your land," he said, "that do not believe the same way you do. They do not keep your laws. You should have them destroyed. All you need to do is write the decree. I will handle the rest of it."

King Ahasuerus trusted Haman so much that he agreed. "If you think that is best, Haman, you may use whatever you need to do it." He gave Haman his ring as a sign of permission.

Filled with evil glee, Haman rushed to send out the message. Throughout all the lands the news was posted:

"Destroy all Jews, both young and old, in one day on the thirteenth day of the twelfth month and take the spoil of them for a profit."

When the Jews learned of the decree, they tore their clothes and mourned loudly. They dressed themselves in sackcloth and put ashes on their heads, praying that the Lord God would save them.

Queen Esther didn't know about the decree until a servant came with the news. "The man Mordecai stands outside the king's gate in sackcloth and ashes," he told the queen.

"Something is dreadfully wrong," Esther said as she quickly gathered some clothes. "Take these to him," she said. "Tell him to put them on."

But the servant returned. "Mordecai would not put on the clothes," he said.

Esther sent for a trusted messenger. "I must know why Mordecai is mourning," she said. "Please find out for me."

The messenger returned from the king's gate. "Mordecai tells me that Haman has commanded that all the Jews be destroyed," he said. "Here is proof of it." He held up the copy of the decree that Mordecai had given him. "Mordecai says you must go to the king and beg for the lives of your people."

Esther gasped. "I cannot! The only time I can go before the king is when he sends for me. He has not sent for me for thirty days. If I go before him and he does not hold out his golden scepter, that will mean death for me!"

Again Mordecai sent a message. "Esther, if you do not speak to the king, the Lord will deliver His people anyway, but you will be punished. Who knows but that you may have become queen just for such a time as this?"

Esther sighed. "Send this message to Mordecai," she said. "Tell all the Jews to fast and pray for me for three days and three nights. At the end of that time I will go to the king, even though it may mean my death. But if I perish, I perish."

Mordecai did everything Esther said. He prayed, all the other Jews prayed, and Esther prayed for guidance and wisdom. Esther also prayed that the Lord would prepare the king's heart.

A Banquet for Three

At the end of three days, Esther prepared to go before the king. She dressed just as she knew the king liked her to dress. She walked slowly through the courtyard and through the inner court. There, in the royal house, she could see King Ahasuerus sitting on his royal throne. He looked up and saw Esther. Esther felt her heart beating hard.

"O God of my fathers," she whispered, "be with me now. Give me wisdom in my actions and in my words."

Esther stood in the doorway, her head bowed low in reverence to the king. King Ahasuerus watched the queen. He knew that she was facing death to approach him. The servants dared not breathe.

Then the king held out the golden scepter for her to touch, his sign that he accepted her.

The servants sighed with relief. Esther sighed too and smiled as she approached her husband.

Ahasuerus smiled back at her. "What is your request, Queen Esther? I will give you whatever you want, up to half of my kingdom."

Esther spoke softly. "If it please you, Your Majesty," she said, "I would like to invite Your Majesty and Haman to a banquet."

The king listened in amazement. Esther had risked her life for this! Quickly he called his servants. "Tell Haman that Queen Esther is having a banquet for us. Tell him to come immediately."

When Haman heard the message, he clapped his
hands together in delight. An invitation to eat with
the king and the queen! He hurried to Esther's
banquet as quickly as he could.

King Ahasuerus enjoyed the banquet so much that
he said, "Esther, whatever you want, I will give you.
Just ask."

Still Esther was careful. "I would like for you and
Haman to come to another banquet tomorrow night."

Haman was delighted. "I am the favorite of the
king," he thought to himself as he left the palace.
"And I am the favorite of the queen! Who is nobler
than Haman? No one! No one!"

As Haman passed through the gates, he smiled to himself. All the people were bowing, as always.

But . . . there was Mordecai! Still he would not bow. Haman clenched his fists. He forgot all the exciting things that had happened to him. All he could think about was this man Mordecai.

With effort Haman kept himself from doing anything to Mordecai just then. He went home as fast as he could and called everyone around.

"Listen to me," he said. "I have been honored above all men! The queen held a banquet for the king tonight, and I was the only other one invited. Moreover, she is holding another banquet for me tomorrow night!" Haman stood tall and proud.

All his friends and family stood speechless with wonder. No one they had ever known had received such an honor.

"But still," Haman said as his face suddenly turned red with anger, "this doesn't satisfy me as long as I see the man Mordecai sitting at the gate."

"You are letting this Mordecai ruin your happiness." Haman's wife shook her finger at him. "You are not just anyone. You are the chief of princes. You are the one who went to the queen's banquet. You are Haman! Do not let Mordecai distress you. This very night, command that a tall gallows be built, taller than any in the land. Tomorrow ask the king's permission to hang Mordecai on that gallows. Everyone knows that the king will do anything you suggest, Haman. Then you can enjoy the banquet with a merry heart."

Haman's eyes narrowed into slits. "Yes," he said. "Of course. I will do that very thing!"

Rescue

That night the king couldn't sleep. He commanded that a servant bring something to read to him.

The servant read from the chronicles of the king. For hours his sleepy voice droned on and on. King Ahasuerus still lay awake. Then as morning began to dawn, the servant read a very interesting story. It was about two men who had plotted to kill the king. The man Mordecai had reported it and had saved the king's life.

King Ahasuerus sat up in his bed. "I remember that. Read to me what has been done for this noble man. I am sure it was something great."

"There is no record that anything has been done," the servant replied. "Mordecai was never rewarded."

"Never rewarded?" King Ahasuerus said slowly. "How did that happen? I must surely do something for him." He looked around, thinking he heard a noise in the outer court. "Who is there?"

"It is Haman, Your Majesty," the servant answered. "He has come to see Your Majesty on urgent business."

"Send him in immediately. I have some important business to discuss with him too."

Haman came bustling into the king's bedroom. He was eager to ask if he could hang Mordecai. He wanted to hurry and get the hanging over with early so that he could enjoy the banquet that night.

But before he could speak a word of request, King Ahasuerus said, "Haman, what will I do for a man I am delighted to honor?"

Haman felt lightheaded and dizzy. He thought to himself, "The king must want to honor me. Who else could it be? This will be the most glorious day of my life." Then he spoke his wish, a wish he had been dreaming of for some time.

"Your Majesty, if you delight to honor a special man, this is my suggestion. Give him your cloak to wear and your horse to ride, and put your crown on his head. Then send one of your most noble princes to lead this special man on horseback through the city. The noble prince will shout before him, 'This is what will be done for the man that the king delights to honor!' "

King Ahasuerus smiled. "That is an excellent idea. And since you are my most noble prince, you are the one who will do it. Hurry and do this very thing for Mordecai the Jew. Be sure to do all that you suggested."

Mordecai! Haman tried hard not to let the king
see the look on his face. Now he could never ask
permission to hang Mordecai on the gallows. Never!

Haman quickly left the palace. For fear of his life, he did everything the king had told him to do. He gave Mordecai the royal cloak, the royal horse, and the royal crown. And then Haman went through the street shouting, "This is what will be done for the man that the king delights to honor!"

Then Haman ran home, mourning loudly over what had happened.

"This is not a good sign," his wife said. "If this happened with Mordecai the Jew, it is a sign that something worse is going to happen."

"Something worse!" Haman shouted. "Nothing could possibly happen that is any worse than what happened to me today."

As he was speaking, the king's servant came in to remind him of Queen Esther's banquet. Haman hurried away.

That evening, just as the evening before, King Ahasuerus asked Queen Esther what he could do for her.

"O King," Esther answered, "if it pleases you, let my life and the lives of my people be spared. A wicked man is planning to kill us."

King Ahasuerus felt shocked and angry that someone would try to kill his queen. "Who is this man that dares plot such a thing?" he asked.

"My enemy and the enemy of all my people is this wicked Haman!" Esther's finger pointed straight at the astonished man.

Haman—the king's favorite! King Ahasuerus was so upset that he left the room without a word.

Haman collapsed in terror. He had not known that Queen Esther was a Jewess. Now he remembered his wife's dark words and begged Queen Esther to spare his life.

The king returned and, full of anger, shouted at Haman. A servant said, "Haman has built a gallows where he is planning to hang Mordecai."

"He wants to hang Mordecai, the man who saved my life? That is enough. Hang Haman on that gallows."

So Haman was hanged. Then King Ahasuerus did what was needed to rescue the Jews. The appointed day became a day of feasting and gladness instead of a day of death and mourning.

Mordecai was made the chief of all the princes, the very position that Haman used to have. Esther had been made the queen "for such a time as this."

Days to Remember

New Year in a New Land

Karen Wilt

illustrated by Stephanie True, Kathy Pflug, and Janet Davis

The Old Ways

Sonya walked quickly past the doors of the other apartments.

"Hello," called Mrs. Tallman cheerfully.

Sonya glanced up at her neighbor standing in her doorway. "Hello," she said shyly. She edged toward the stairs that led to her own apartment.

"How do you like living in America?" Mrs. Tallman asked.

"It's . . . fine," Sonya said and put her foot on the first step.

Mrs. Tallman smiled at her, but Sonya turned and darted up the stairs.

Outside her apartment, she paused to touch the little brass mezuzah box. A tiny scroll had been folded inside it. Sonya had never seen it, but she knew by heart the commandments written on it. She remembered the day Papa had unhooked it from their apartment door in Russia. She thought about their dangerous journey to America. Here they didn't have to be afraid anymore. But Sonya always was.

"Who is there?" Rachel called. "Sonya, is that you at the door?"

Sonya slipped inside and closed the door. Jacob sat at the table with his schoolbooks spread out in front of him.

"Boo!" Rachel said, jumping from behind the door.

Sonya giggled and gave Rachel a hug.

"Please clear off the table for dinner, Jacob," Mama said.

Quickly Sonya and Rachel set the plates on the table. Then Sonya heard Papa's heavy footsteps on the stairs.

As he opened the door, the girls pounced on him. He swept them off their feet with a big bear hug.

But at supper Papa sat quietly, listening to everyone else talk. When Mama started to clear the table, he stopped her.

"We must talk," he said. Mama sat down again. "Children, we did not have much in Russia. Many times we were hungry." Papa looked at each of them. "Now I have a good job here in America. But I do not get paid for several weeks. We must be careful with the money we brought with us."

He stopped to look at Sonya's face. "This Sabbath day is the Jewish New Year. We have no money to buy fruit and honey to celebrate. This year we will just have each other."

"That is enough," Mama said.

Rachel and Jacob nodded, but as hard as she tried, Sonya could not keep back a tear. It slid down her cheek before she could hide it.

"Now, Sonya," Papa said. "Next year we will have a great feast."

"Oh, Papa, I'm glad we have each other," Sonya said, putting her arms around his neck. "But I miss our old friends and the old ways in Russia."

Mama patted Sonya's arm. "She is young, Papa," Mama said. "Now, whose turn is it to help with the dishes?"

"Mine, Mama," Rachel said.

Papa talked to Sonya as Mama and Rachel cleared the table. At last Sonya tiptoed off to bed.

Rachel sat down across from Jacob as he spread out his books again.

"I wish we could have a New Year's feast for Sonya," she said.

Jacob put his pencil down. "The Tallmans have always been very friendly. We could ask Mr. Tallman if he needs help in his market. Maybe we could get enough for a little New Year's feast."

"Jacob, what a good idea!" Rachel said excitedly. "Let's ask Papa if we may!"

Sonya's New Year's Feast

Jacob swept the storeroom while Rachel dusted
the shelves. Then they put cans on the shelves.

"Well, I see the Lord has sent me some hard
workers," Mr. Tallman said as they put away their
aprons. "You may work every afternoon for one hour."

Jacob and Rachel grinned at each other. "Payday is
next Tuesday," he said. He turned back to his register.
He did not see them look at each other in dismay.
Tuesday would be after the New Year! Sonya would
not have her feast after all!

Just then the bell on the door jingled and Sonya peeked in.

"Rachel," she whispered in Russian, "Mama wants you to bring home a box of salt."

"Hello," said Mr. Tallman. "Who is this?"

Rachel pulled Sonya in the door. "This is Sonya, Mr. Tallman. She is our sister."

"Oh, yes, my wife has told me about young Sonya," Mr. Tallman said. He smiled at Sonya's surprised look. He picked up a shiny red apple and placed it in her hand. "Go ahead and eat it," he said.

Sonya looked at the apple. Then she looked up at Mr. Tallman. "If you please, may I take it home?"

Puzzled, Mr. Tallman asked, "Why not eat it here?"

"Sonya is thinking about the New Year's feast, Mr. Tallman," said Rachel. "That is why we wanted to get jobs—so we could buy apples and honey for the feast."

Mr. Tallman leaned against the counter, thinking. "And Tuesday payday is after the New Year," he said.

Slowly, Jacob and Rachel nodded.

"Well," Mr. Tallman smiled. "Whose store is this? Mine! I can have payday any time I want, can't I?"

208

Jacob began to smile. Rachel and Sonya looked up with wide eyes at Mr. Tallman.

"Now," Mr. Tallman said, looking at Sonya. "You are Sonya Kuril, and you have a sister, Rachel, and a brother, Jacob." He pretended to count on his fingers. "And a mother and a father, that makes five."

Mr. Tallman picked up his note pad. "This will do," he said. He wrote on the pad for a minute. Sonya looked at Jacob. He raised his eyes and shrugged his shoulders.

Then Mr. Tallman ripped off the page and handed it to Sonya. "Can you read English?" he asked.

"Yes, sir," Sonya replied.

"Read it out loud," Jacob said, trying to peek over her arm.

"Give to Sonya five apples, a bunch of grapes, and a bag of oranges . . . ," Sonya said. She stopped in amazement.

"Keep going," Rachel poked her.

"And a jar of honey!" Sonya said.

"For the New Year," Mr. Tallman said. "Rachel and Jacob are such good workers that I am giving them part of their money ahead of time. What is left I will give them on the regular payday, Tuesday."

"Why would you do this?" asked Jacob. "You are not Jewish."

"No," replied Mr. Tallman, "but I am a Christian. Jesus teaches that we should give of what we have to the strangers in our midst. And you are strangers to our land, aren't you?" he added with a twinkle in his eye.

Jacob nodded thoughtfully. "I have heard Papa say that you believe Jesus was the Messiah. I would like to hear more about that. I think Papa would too."

"I will talk to your father," said Mr. Tallman. "But for now, we need to fill Sonya's order."

He picked up a bag and filled it with fruit. Then he put a jar of honey on top.

Even Sonya waved happily as they left the market. The three sang as they walked up the stairs to their apartment.

Sonya stopped in front of the door to touch the mezuzah box. "I think I like this new land," she said. "I think it will be a good year after all!"

Up in the Air

Gail Fitzgerald
illustrated by
Sam Laterza

It's 1783. You want to take an exciting ride. What will you choose to ride in? No, you can't go in a rocket, for they haven't been invented yet. How about boarding a sleek silver jet? You forgot again; it's only 1783. Men are not even thinking about jets yet. So what are they dreaming about?

All through history man has dreamed of flying like a bird. Sometimes people even made wings for themselves and tried to fly. They climbed to high places and jumped off.

Each one went crashing to the ground. Still, men dreamed on and on.

212

Joseph Montgolfier was one Frenchman who kept dreaming. One day he was thinking about the clouds floating in the air. "Those clouds look like the steam that comes from our kitchen kettle," he said to himself.

Joseph hurried home, put the kettle over the fire, and waited impatiently. As the steam came out, Joseph tried to capture it in a paper bag. The bag fell to the floor.

"Hmmm," Joseph said to his brother and sister, "clouds are like smoke too. Let's fill a paper bag with smoke."

Quickly they threw straw on the kitchen fire. As the smoke rose, the paper bag expanded. The heat of the air in the bag made it rise to the ceiling!

That floating hot-air bag was the beginning of balloons. Now perhaps you're thinking of the brightly colored balloons you get at a circus or fair. You must think larger, like Joseph did. He began to dream of hot-air balloons big enough to carry people.

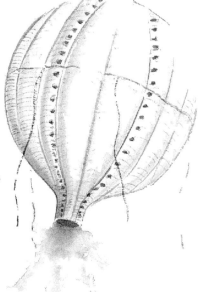

Much experimenting had to be done before balloons could carry people. In 1783 Joseph Montgolfier made the first real balloon. As a large, excited crowd watched, Montgolfier filled his silk balloon with hot air. Strong men had to hold the ropes to keep the balloon from floating away. At last Montgolfier gave the signal, the men let go, and the balloon floated up. The crowd cheered. The first balloon was off!

The king of France heard about Montgolfier's balloon and asked him to make a special one. The day finally came when the huge, beautiful balloon was ready. It had a willow basket underneath that was big enough for someone to ride in.

"No one is going to ride in the balloon," the king ordered. "It's too dangerous."

But the king did allow a sheep, a duck, and a rooster to take the first ride. The balloon took off with the sheep bleating, the duck quacking, and the rooster crowing. When the balloon finally landed, all three animals were found safe and sound. The rooster did, however, have a broken wing from being kicked by the sheep.

The success of that balloon made Montgolfier want to keep on experimenting. He made a balloon as tall as a seven-story building! The big basket underneath had enough room for two men, straw and wool for the fire, and a fire pan. But Montgolfier didn't want to take the first ride!

Two men volunteered eagerly for the job. One man was to put the straw and wool on the fire. The other man was to be the navigator. November 21, 1783, was clear and sunny. As the first balloon with men in it took off, all of Paris watched. Women shouted, men cheered, and children waved. Higher and higher went the balloon as the men added fuel to the fire. When the men became too interested in watching the scenery, the fire began to die down.

The balloon dropped until the men noticed their danger. Quickly they threw more fuel on the fire, and the balloon floated back up into the sky. Finally, after twenty-five minutes, the supply of fuel gave out. The balloon floated to the ground. It had traveled five miles from its launching pad in Paris.

After that, many people experimented with balloons. Some men put oars, sails, and rudders on their balloons. That didn't work. Others filled their balloons with hydrogen instead of hot air. And that did work.

As time passed, scientists used balloons to collect information about air currents and the weather. Generals used hot-air balloons in war to see where the enemy was. People rode in balloons just because they were fun! Do you think riding in a balloon would be fun?

Danger on the Mountain

Karen Wooster

illustrated by Stephanie True, Janet Davis, and Johanna Berg

A New Puppy

Hansel carried his armload of firewood into the kitchen. "Your first spring in the mountains has certainly been a cold one, Hansel." Grandmother shivered as he dropped the firewood into the wooden box near the stove. She smiled at him. "Make sure the back door is closed tightly."

Hansel pushed hard on the door. "When is Grandfather coming home?" he asked.

Grandmother glanced at the old clock above the table. "He wanted to get his letter to your aunt in the two o'clock post," she said. "Then he stopped at the pastor's house. They probably got to talking as always. He'll be along soon."

Hansel rubbed a circle on the windowpane and peered out. "Here he comes now! He has a big basket with him."

Hansel hurried to open the door.

"What's that, Grandfather?" Hansel asked.

Grandfather's eyes twinkled. "Oh, just a little something for you," he said.

Grandmother wiped her hands and came to look over their shoulders as Grandfather put the basket on the floor.

The covering on the basket quivered, and a soft nose appeared under the edge of the rough cloth. Then the covering slid and a puppy sat up, the edge of the cloth draped over one eye.

"A puppy! For me?" Hansel exclaimed, gathering the puppy up in his arms.

"That's what Pastor said—just for you." Grandfather smiled. "He's a Saint Bernard, and he's an orphan. His mother died when he was born, so we will have to take special care of him, just like we will of you. What do you think of him?"

"He's terrific!" Hansel grinned happily as the puppy wiggled and licked his face.

"And just what are you going to call this fine puppy?" asked Grandmother. "He should have a special name."

Hansel held the puppy still enough to gaze into his brown eyes. "You remind me of a bear cub," he said. "I will call you Bear."

Grandmother gave Hansel a hug. "That's a fine name," she said. "Now I'll find him a warm corner while you go get ready for supper."

Bear

As the months went by, Bear grew bigger and bigger. Soon he didn't look like a puppy anymore. Through the spring and summer, Hansel and Bear played together. Hansel grew strong and brown in the sun. Bear just grew!

Hansel's friend Markus liked Bear too. The boys and Bear spent many long summer hours racing through the woods and along the green slopes of the mountain.

"I declare," said Grandmother. "I don't think those three have left a stone unturned on this mountain!"

Grandfather nodded. "You're probably right," he said. Then he added, "It's good for them to know the land. When winter comes, they will need to know what lies hidden under the snow."

Grandmother nodded. "I always fear to see the children ski down the mountain to school."

"That's the way it has always been, Mother," said Grandfather. "We must teach Hansel what we can and then just trust the Lord to take care of him."

As autumn drew closer, Grandfather went with Hansel and Markus more often. He taught them where the safe ski trails would be when snow blanketed the land. He showed them dangerous spots where snowdrifts would pile up over their heads. And everywhere they went, Bear followed.

Soon September came, and it was time to go to school in the valley. Every day Hansel walked down the slope to Markus's house. Together they walked the rest of the way down the mountain to school. In the afternoons, Bear met Hansel at Markus's house. He and Hansel would race the rest of the way home.

The leaves changed color and fell from the trees. The boys waxed their skis and began exercising to make their ankles stronger. Bear sniffed the strange boards tied to the boys' feet.

"Oh, Bear," cried Hansel. "Watch out!"

For the second time Bear had run in front of him as he practiced walking on the skis.

Markus laughed as Hansel landed in a heap on top of Bear.

But soon Bear got used to the strange boards the boys called skis. At last the day came that the boys had been waiting for.

Hansel came running in from the barn one evening. "It's snowing! It's snowing!" he called.

Grandfather looked up from his leatherwork. "Yes," he said. "There will be a lot of snow on the ground by morning."

"Enough to ski to school?" asked Hansel eagerly.

"Enough to ski to school," said Grandfather.

The Storm

The next morning Hansel put on his coat, hat, and mittens. He strapped his school pack onto his back. Grandmother went to the door to watch Hansel buckle on his skis.

Bear was too busy playing with the funny white stuff on the ground to pay attention to the skis this morning. He jumped and rolled in the snow. Then he tried to run, plowing through the snow and sending sprays of powdery snow over everyone.

"Be careful, Bear." Hansel laughed. "I don't want to have to dig you out! I must be at school before eight."

They prayed together for safety; then Grandmother and Grandfather waved goodbye as Hansel skied down the slope to Markus's house. Bear romped through the snow after him.

Grandfather looked down at Grandmother's worried face. "Now, Mother," he said, "let's just leave it with the Lord."

Each morning the boys skied to school. Each afternoon, Bear met them at Markus's house. The days went by quickly.

One morning, Grandfather looked at the sky and shook his head. "Bad weather may be coming," he said. "Be careful today, Son."

"I will, Grandfather," said Hansel. Before he left the house, he and his grandparents had their usual time of prayer. Then Hansel left for school. Bear followed but came back later, whining softly. Then he lay down outside, facing the ski trail.

By noon the sky had turned a flat gray. The teacher dismissed school early. Hansel and Markus strapped their skis to their backs and hurried up the trail, while keeping watchful eyes on the darkening sky.

Suddenly Markus called, "Wait, Hansel!"

Hansel turned back. Markus was down on one knee, holding his ankle. Hansel stopped beside him just as snow began to fall. "I've twisted my ankle," said Markus. "I was looking at the sky and stumbled over that rock."

"Do you think your ankle's broken?" Hansel asked, kneeling beside Markus.

"I don't think so," Markus said. He stood up slowly, holding onto Hansel to steady himself. "But I can't walk very well. What can we do?"

Rescue

Snow fell faster, swirling around Markus and Hansel. The icy flakes stung their faces.

Markus hobbled on his ankle. "Go on, Hansel. You can get help."

"No, I can't leave you out here," Hansel replied. "They'll send help when we don't get home on time."

"But we left school early today," said Markus. "They won't know! They'll think we are safe at school."

By now they could no longer see more than a few feet in front of them.

"We must remember what Grandfather taught us," said Hansel. "We must find shelter through the storm."

Hansel helped Markus to the shelter of some overhanging rocks that Grandfather had pointed out so long ago. They huddled close together to keep warm.

They talked for a while about different things and then sat, trying to peer through the white curtain of snow.

"We'll be all right, Markus," said Hansel. "I know we will."

"How can you know?" Markus asked. "We might never be found!"

"Because we prayed for safety just this morning," said Hansel. "And I know the Lord will take care of us."

Markus nodded. "Yes, I know the Lord answers prayer."

For a moment the boys didn't speak. They stared out into the whirling snow. Then without looking at Hansel, Markus spoke quietly. "But I'm still afraid."

"So am I," Hansel said slowly. "Let's pray and ask the Lord to give us courage and to help Grandfather to find us quickly."

Both boys bowed their heads and began to pray.

The snow piled higher and higher on the mountain.

At the house, Bear raced back and forth, whining and scratching at the door.

Grandfather nodded. "I know how you feel, Bear. And I know what we can both do about it."

Grandmother got warm clothing for him while he went to the porch to get rope and snowshoes.

Grandfather tied the rope carefully to Bear and put on the snowshoes. Then he and Bear walked out into the white storm.

The icy wind whipped at them, but Grandfather bent his head and held onto the rope. Bear trudged through the snow, moving slowly down the trail.

Then as they passed the barn, the swirling snow lessened, and Grandfather could see ahead of him. He felt a tug on the rope as Bear, too, moved ahead more freely. Grandfather strained to see farther along the trail in front of him, but all he could see were the outlines of the tall evergreens that bordered the trail. He and Bear moved slowly along the trees. As they neared the overhanging rocks, Bear stopped and raised his head. He barked and swung off the trail.

"Good boy," said Grandfather, moving with the dog. They found the boys huddled under the rocks.

"Bear!" Hansel sat up as the excited dog licked his face. "You came, Grandfather!"

Grandfather looked at Markus's ankle, then lifted Markus onto his back.

"We are all right, Hansel," Markus said. "Just like you said we would be. The Lord helped your grandfather to find us."

"And He gave us courage when we were afraid," said Hansel.

Ahead of them Bear gave a short bark. "Come on," he seemed to say. "Come on!"

Professor Plumcott's Problem

Susan W. Young
illustrated by Tim Banks

A Puzzling Predicament

It was a fine day when Professor Plumcott was elected mayor of Plumville. The birds were singing, the sun was shining, the flowers were in full bloom, and the people were smiling and cheering. Everyone knew that Professor Plumcott was the man for the job—everyone, that is, but Professor Plumcott himself.

Professor Plumcott was worried. He did not mind being the mayor. In fact, he rather liked the idea.

He did not mind wearing a suit and tie and looking important. He did not mind meeting the people, shaking their hands, and kissing their babies. He did not mind talking to them when he met them on the street or in a store. But there was one thing that had him worried.

Long before Professor Plumcott became the mayor of Plumville it had been decided that once a week the mayor would give a speech to all the people of Plumville. The people would gather in front of the courthouse to hear the speech. The speech would be about something important, a speech that only a mayor could make. But Mayor Plumcott did not want to make a speech only a mayor could make. He did not want to make a speech at all. He did not know what to say.

But there was time. There was time for Professor Plumcott to think of something to say before the day came for his speech. He decided to look in the town, up one road and down the next. He would look at the buildings and in the streets. He would listen to the sounds the people made. He would think and think. He would think of something to say.

Finally the day came. The people of Plumville gathered at the courthouse steps waiting for the mayor to speak. Mayor Plumcott still did not know what to say. He looked at the men and the women and the children. He looked at the blue sky and the green grass. He looked all around, but he could think of nothing to say. Then he had an idea.

"People of Plumville," he said, leaning forward and pointing his finger, "do you know what I am going to say to you today?"

"No!" said all the people as they shook their heads.

"Are you sure you do not know?" Mayor Plumcott acted surprised.

The people shook their heads again. "No," they repeated.

"Then it would be a waste of my time for me to speak to people who do not know anything at all about this important matter. It is of no use for me to talk to people who know nothing."

With that Mayor Plumcott turned on his heel and disappeared into the courthouse. He wiped his brow with his big white handkerchief. No one knew he did not know what to say.

Another week passed, and again it was time for Mayor Plumcott to speak to the people. Again he did not know what to say.

"Oh, what am I to do?" he said to himself as he dressed that morning. "Why can I not think of anything to say? I think I am a fine mayor. I kiss the babies and shake the people's hands and stop to talk when I pass them on the street, but when it comes to giving a speech, I cannot think of what to say. But I cannot be late, so I must be on my way."

The people stood before the courthouse steps, every man, woman, and child of Plumville. They

were waiting for him to say something only a mayor could say. But Mayor Plumcott had nothing to say.

Mayor Plumcott mounted the steps of the courthouse one by one. He read the words printed over the doors at the top of the steps. He looked at the colors in the stained glass windows. He counted the bricks in the courthouse wall. He still could think of nothing to say.

He turned to face the people. "People of Plumville," he said, "do you know what I want to say to you today?" He folded his hands behind his back. "Do you know what I am going to say?"

The people stood still. They remembered last week when they had said no. They looked at one another and nodded their heads. "Yes! Yes, we do," they said together.

"You do know what I am going to say?" The mayor crossed his arms. "Then there is no reason why I should say it. I would not want to bore you by telling you something you already know." And with that he turned and walked away.

A Personal Promise

The next week passed too quickly for Mayor Plumcott. All week long he had thought and thought and he had searched and searched, but he still had nothing to say, nothing that only a mayor would say. The day for his speech came and the time drew near. He climbed the steps of the courthouse as slowly as he could.

"Good people of Plumville," he said, standing tall, "do you know what I am going to say to you today?"

The people said nothing at all. The men said nothing. The women said nothing. The children just stared.

The mayor of Plumville looked at each face. Still no one spoke. He took a deep breath. "People of Plumville," he said as he smoothed his coat, "I see that today you have nothing to say." He swallowed hard. "Are you sure you have nothing to say?" The Mayor wiped his brow. He cleared his throat. "People of Plumville, I, too, have nothing to say."

The people of Plumville began to smile, and then they began to cheer. They knew that Mayor Plumcott was the best mayor of all. They were tired of mayors who made speeches about important matters they could not understand. They were tired of mayors who made long speeches when they really had nothing at all to say.

Suddenly Mayor Plumcott thought of something
to say. "Since I am the mayor and I think you'll
agree, I hereby declare that there will be no more
speeches, at least not one every week. From now on
when I think of something important to say, I will
tell you." He walked down the steps and out through
the crowd. He shook hands with the men, smiled at
the women, and kissed the babies. And to each
person he had something to say.

Raised from the Dead

(A choral reading taken from John 11:1-46)

unattributed

illustrated by Keith Neely

Readers

BOYS
Boy 1: Narrator
Boy 2: Jesus
Boys Chorus

GIRLS
Girl A: Narrator
Girl B: Martha
Girl C: Mary
Girls Chorus

Boy 1:   Now a certain man was sick, named Lazarus, of Bethany, the town of Mary and her sister, Martha.

Girls: Therefore his sisters sent unto Jesus, saying

Girl B and Girl C: Lord, behold, he whom thou lovest is sick.

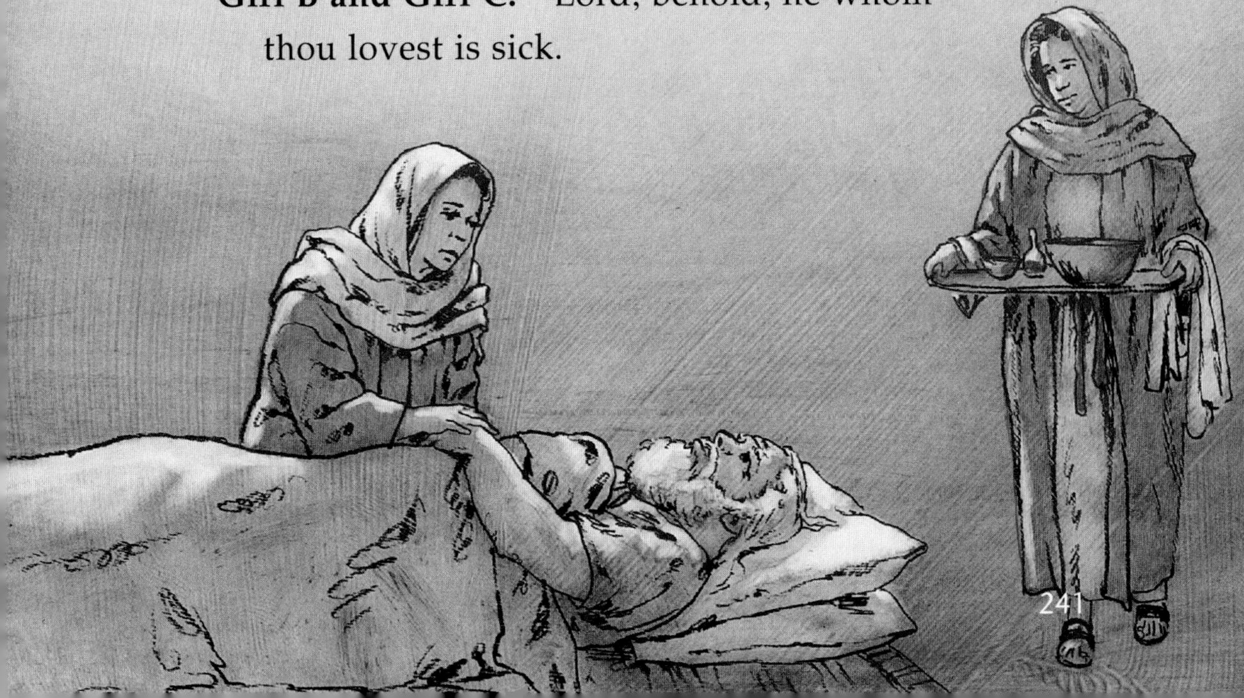

Boys: When Jesus heard that, he said,

Boy 2: This sickness is not unto death, but for the glory of God, that the Son of God might be glorified thereby.

All: That the Son of God might be glorified thereby.

Girls: Now Jesus loved Martha, and her sister, and Lazarus.

Boys: When he had heard therefore that Lazarus was sick, he abode two days still in the same place where he was.

Boy 1:   And after that he saith,

Boy 2:   Our friend Lazarus sleepeth; but I go, that I may awake him out of sleep.

Boys: Then when Jesus came, he found that Lazarus had lain in the grave four days already.

Girl B: Then Martha, as soon as she heard that Jesus was coming, went and met him:

Girl C: But Mary sat still in the house.

Girls: Then said Martha unto Jesus,

Girl B: Lord, if thou hadst been here, my brother had not died. But I know, that even now, whatsoever thou wilt ask of God, God will give it thee.

All: God will give it thee.

Boy 1:   Jesus saith unto her,

Boy 2:   Thy brother shall rise again.

243

Girl A: When Mary was come where Jesus was and saw him, she fell down at his feet, saying unto him,

Girl C: Lord, if thou hadst been here, my brother had not died.

Boys: When Jesus therefore saw her weeping, and the Jews also weeping which came with her, he groaned in the spirit and was troubled, and said,

Boy 2: Where have ye laid him?

Boys: They said unto him,

All: Lord, come and see.

Girls: *(sadly)* Jesus wept.

Girl C: Behold how he loved him!

Girls: Behold how he loved him!

All: Behold how he loved him!

Boys: Jesus therefore again groaning in himself cometh to the grave. It was a cave, and a stone lay upon it.

Boy 2:   Take ye away the stone.

All: Then they took away the stone from the place where the dead was laid.

Boy 1:   And Jesus lifted up his eyes, and said,

Boy 2:   Father, I thank thee that thou hast heard me. And I knew that thou hearest me always; but because of the people which stand by I said it, that they may believe that thou hast sent me.

All: That they may believe that thou hast sent me.

Boy 1:   And when he thus had spoken, he cried with a loud voice,

Boy 2:   Lazarus, come forth.

All: *(quietly, like an echo)* Lazarus, come forth.

Girls: And he that was dead

All: *(joyfully)* came forth,

Girl A: *(with excitement)* bound hand and foot with grave clothes; and his face was bound about with a napkin.

Boy 1:   Jesus saith unto them,

Boy 2:   Loose him, and let him go.

Boys: Then many of the Jews which came to Mary,

Girls: and had seen the things which Jesus did,

All: believed on him.

Space Walk
Karen Wilt

For months Major White and Commander McDivitt trained every day. They learned to float in space. They learned to use an air gun to move in space. Now their training would be put to use. Today Major White would be the first American to walk in space!

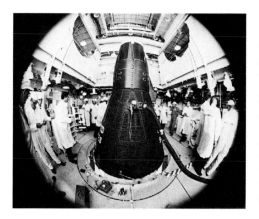

On June 3, 1965, *Gemini IV* stood on the launching pad. At 4:10 in the morning, Major White and Commander McDivitt woke up. Liftoff time would be 9:00 A.M.

As the two men prepared for the flight, scientists moved quickly about the launching pad. The huge rocket was checked and re-checked.

At last Major White and Commander McDivitt were ready. An elevator carried them up to start their journey. The elevator stopped at the hatch of the huge spaceship. The astronauts climbed in and buckled up their safety harnesses.

The big tower beside the rocket lowered. But it stopped before it reached the ground. Then it was raised up to the hatch again. Something was wrong!

The scientists went to work. After a careful search, they found a connector that had been put in wrong. As quickly as possible, a workman repaired it.

Mission Control set a new liftoff time—10:16 A.M.

The astronauts were ready. The rocket engines hummed—10, 9, 8, 7, 6, 5, 4, 3, 2, 1, blastoff!

Gemini IV lifted into the air with a thunderous roar.

Inside the spacecraft, Major White and Commander McDivitt couldn't hear the rumbling blast of the engines, but they felt the rocket soar into the sky.

Gemini IV climbed out of the earthbound spectators' sight and started to circle the earth.

The first stage of the rocket fell off. All the fuel inside had been burned up as they blasted off. Later the second stage fell off when its fuel was gone.

Commander McDivitt read a checklist. He marked off each thing that had to be done before Major White's space walk.

Major White put his air gun together. He tied the air gun to his arm and hooked an oxygen tube to his suit. Now he was ready for the space walk!

Back on earth, Mission Control told him to go ahead.

Major White tried to unlatch the hatchway. It wouldn't budge. He tugged until it opened a crack. Then he heaved and pushed until it slid back.

Slowly he climbed out into space. He floated beside the hatchway for a moment.

Then he pointed the air gun downward. He pulled the trigger. The thrust of air from the gun pushed him up the side of the spacecraft. As Major White walked across the spacecraft, the Commander heard the thump, thump of his space boots. Major White rolled down the other side of the spacecraft. He drifted down to Commander McDivitt's window. The Commander snapped his picture.

Then Major White rolled over and faced the earth. The beautiful world shone below him. His voice came over the radio, describing what he saw. "I can sit out here and see the whole California coast," he said.

He rolled over two more times before his air gun ran out of fuel.

"Back in, come on," the Commander said.

"I'm not coming in," Major White laughed.

"Come on, get back in here before it gets dark," the Commander said.

"Okay, I'm going to come into the house," said Major White. He glanced at planet Earth once more. "This is the saddest day of my life," he said as he drifted through the hatchway.

Major White tugged at the hatch as he slipped into his chair. It wouldn't lock. He tugged harder. As he pulled, he floated out of his seat. Commander McDivitt grabbed his legs and dragged him back. The lock clicked into place.

Major White's walk in space had lasted twenty-one minutes.

Gemini IV orbited the earth sixty-two times. Then the Commander fired the retrorockets. The two astronauts heard the bang, bang, bang, bang as the rockets exploded into action. *Gemini IV* turned back to earth. Their journey into space was over. The big spaceship plunged back to the earth.

In just a few minutes, the rocket splashed into the sea.

A helicopter spotted Major White and Commander McDivitt. It picked them up and took them to the aircraft carrier *Wasp*.

The space walk had been a success.

Later the Commander stopped to talk to a newsman. "I did not see God looking into my space cabin window," he said, "as I did not see God looking into my car's windshield on earth. But I could recognize His work in the stars as well as when walking among the flowers in a garden. If you can be with God on earth, you can be with God in space."

Thanksgiving Day

Lydia Maria Child
illustrated by Kathy Pflug

Over the river and through the wood,
To grandfather's house we go;
The horse knows the way
To carry the sleigh
Through the white and drifted snow.

Over the river and through the wood—
Oh, how the wind does blow!
It stings the toes
And bites the nose,
As over the ground we go.

. . . .

Over the river and through the wood
Trot fast, my dapple-gray!
Spring over the ground,
Like a hunting-hound!
For this is Thanksgiving Day.

The Trail West

Milly Howard

illustrated by
Bob Reynolds

*The following story is a
fictional account of the
Lincoln family's move
from Indiana to Illinois.
The incident involving
Abe Lincoln's rescue of
the little dog is true.*

Moving Ahead

A rabbit dashed out of the woods and down the
hill, followed by a yapping little dog. With a flick of
its tail, the rabbit disappeared down a hole. The little
dog trotted around the hole, sniffing. Then, again
yapping loudly, he began to dig. One ear perked up
as he heard children's voices calling in the woods;
then he returned to his frantic digging.

"Dog!" a voice called sternly. A tall, lanky young
man strode out of the woods.

He stopped beside the little dog and looked at the wet dirt scattered around the hole. "Dog," he scolded, shaking his head, "you've been chasing rabbits again. One of these days you're going to get left behind!"

Scooping up the dog, the young man called, "Here he is!"

"Abe found him!" The shout was repeated again in the woods. "Abe found him!"

Soon Abe Lincoln's young nephews and nieces were gathered around him, out of breath from running.

"Chasing rabbits again," said one of the boys, trying to frown at the muddy dog wriggling in Abe's long arms.

"Let me hold him, Abe. I'll keep him from chasing rabbits," said one of the girls.

Abe handed his little dog to his niece. "You mind this time, Dog," he said. "No more trouble from you!"

"Here come the wagons," he said. The children looked up as Abe's father drove the first wagon over the top of the hill. The canvas top swayed as the oxen pulled hard in the mud. Mr. Lincoln cracked his whip and called to the oxen, "Come on, boys!"

Mrs. Lincoln held on to the edge of the wagon seat as they started down the hill toward Abe and the children. Two other wagons followed, those of Dennis Hanks and Levi Hall, Abe's brothers-in-law. Abe's sisters called to their children as the wagons stopped.

"Will we camp here for the night?" Dennis Hanks asked Mr. Lincoln.

"It's a good place," Mr. Lincoln replied, looking around.

Mrs. Lincoln stepped down from the wagon, wrapping her shawl more tightly around her. "Looks like Abe's dog found us a camping place," she said, smiling at Abe.

"He picked a good one," Abe said, nodding toward a stream close by. "There is fresh water."

Abe helped the men unhitch the oxen. Then they went into the forest with their long rifles. It was not long before they came back with a wild turkey. Soon the smoky smell of roasting turkey brought hungry children crowding around the campfire.

Mr. Lincoln thanked God for taking care of them on their long trip across Indiana. Then the cold and weary travelers ate until they were full.

When he was finished, Mr. Lincoln stretched his legs. "Well, I'm tired, but I'm still glad to leave Indiana. This has been a hard winter for us."

"Just think of spring in Illinois," sighed Mrs. Lincoln. "I hope we can plant apple trees."

"We might if you'll bake your apple pies," teased Dennis.

"I hope the farmland is as good as everyone says it is," Levi said. He moved closer to the fire to warm his hands.

"Land that does not have to be cleared sounds fine to me. We'll still have time to plant crops this spring."

"And the game! Deer and bear and everything else! We'll have plenty to eat," Dennis said, and he laughed. "We might even be able to fatten up Abe!"

Abe laughed with the others. His little dog stretched and yawned as Abe rubbed it behind the ears.

"You are right, little dog," said Abe. "It is time for bed."

The next morning the little dog licked Abe's face. Abe opened his eyes. "All right, all right," he said sleepily. "Out you go."

He climbed out of the wagon and set the little dog down. Abe looked around. Ice covered the puddles of water and hung from the tree branches.

"Spring's not here yet, Dog," Abe sighed.

The little dog sniffed the frosty air as he trotted toward the woods. Suddenly a rabbit hopped out of the grass in front of him and dashed between the wagons. With a happy yelp, the chase was on.

Abe laughed as the rabbit stayed just ahead of the little dog. Across the camp they went, back and forth. Then the dog ran too close to the campfire. He bumped the forked branches that held Mrs. Lincoln's pot. Ashes scattered everywhere, and the pot fell down over the dog.

Heads popped out of the wagons. "What is all that racket?"

"Somebody get that dog out of my pot!" called Mrs. Lincoln.

Abe lifted the pot and picked up the little dog.

"See what I told you," he laughed. "Leave those rabbits alone!"

263

With everyone awake, the day's work began. By sunup the wagons were ready to move again. Ice cracked under the oxen's feet as they plodded along. Wagon wheels creaked and rattled west toward Illinois.

Abe and the children walked beside the oxen. The little dog trotted behind them. As the sun rose higher in the sky, the ice melted and made puddles. In the afternoon the wheels of the Lincolns' wagon stuck in the mud. The oxen strained and pulled, but the wagon didn't move.

The other men stopped their wagons to help. They cut branches and dragged small logs from under the trees to pack under the wheels.

Abe climbed onto the wagon seat.

"Hi, Hi! Come on, boys," he shouted, but still the wagon didn't move.

"Wait, Abe," called his father. "Dennis and Levi will help me push behind the wagon."

As the three men pushed, Abe cracked the whip, shouting to the oxen. The little dog ran under the wagon and nipped fiercely at the oxen's heels. The oxen snorted and pulled. The wheels creaked as the wagon began to move.

"Come on, boys," shouted Abe.

The wagon jerked, and mud splashed everywhere. They were out of the hole! The three men wiped mud from their faces.

Abe laughed as he jumped down from the high wagon seat. "I had the best job," he said.

His father picked up the muddy little dog. "Your dog almost got stepped on," he said. "Better put him in the wagon."

Abe cleaned the dog as well as he could before putting him in the wagon. "Stay there, Dog. We have work to do."

Left Behind

That was not the last mud hole on the trail. The travelers went through another and another as the spring rains began to sweep the country. The cold and rain sent the children huddling under the canvas. At night the puddles froze; the next day the sun melted the trail into slush. But everybody was happy. They were going west! The closer they got to Illinois, the more they wanted to go on.

Then one day they came to a stream it did not seem they could cross.

"Do you think we can make it across with the wagons?" Dennis asked, looking at the ice-covered water.

Mr. Lincoln shook his head doubtfully. "It looks dangerous," he said. "Let's see if there is a shallow spot upstream or downstream."

The men walked both directions and looked. There was no better place to cross. They returned to the wagons where their wives waited. The children were playing on the bank, the little dog running at their heels.

"We'll have to cross here," Mr. Lincoln told the women. "Better get the children into the wagons."

Quickly the children climbed into the wagons and sat close to their mothers. They made no sound as the wagons creaked one by one into the water. If the wagons tipped over, everything could be lost!

The thin ice cracked under the oxen's feet. Water rushed around their legs.

"Easy, boys," cried Mr. Lincoln as the wagon swayed. The wagon bumped along slowly as the oxen carefully felt their way. At last they were on the other side of the stream.

"Good boys," called Abe. He and his father jumped down. Abe led the oxen out of the way as the other two wagons splashed by them.

"Look, Uncle Abe," called one of the boys, leaning out the back of a wagon. "There is your little dog!"

268

Abe looked back across the stream. Sure enough, there was his dog! He was dashing back and forth on the other side.

"Why didn't someone put him in the wagon?" asked Levi.

Abe groaned. "I thought the children had him."

"He wasn't with us when we got into the wagons," called one of the girls. "Probably chasing rabbits again!"

"Dog, I told you you'd get left someday," Abe called. "Over here, come over here!"

The little dog whined and looked down at the broken ice, then looked back at Abe.

"He's afraid of the ice, Abe," said his stepmother. "He won't swim."

"We can't help him now," said Mr. Lincoln. "We can't take a wagon back across that stream. It's too dangerous."

"Abe, we've got to go on," said Dennis kindly. "It'll be dark shortly."

One of the girls began to cry. Abe looked at the little dog.

"The wagons can't go across, but a man could," he said thoughtfully.

He sat down and began to pull off his shoes and socks.

"You'll catch your death of cold," cried Mrs. Lincoln.

"I can't leave him there to die," Abe replied as he stepped into the water. Slowly he felt his way through the rushing water. The thin, broken ice swept past his legs. Halfway across the stream he slipped. The people on the shore gasped, but Abe caught himself and moved on, still feeling his way with his bare feet.

When he reached the other side, the happy dog met him, wagging his tail. Abe picked him up and looked across at the other shore. It would be even harder going back. How would he keep the dog still?

Abe thought for a moment, then tucked the dog into his shirt. The little dog lay still as Abe began the crossing again. Slowly, foot by foot, he felt his way through the freezing water. His feet grew numb, until he could barely feel the rocks under them. At last he reached the other shore. The men pulled him up on the bank, and Mrs. Lincoln quickly wrapped him in a blanket.

"Had us worried there for a minute, Abe," Levi said.

"Into that wagon, Abe Lincoln," his stepmother said tearfully. "You're soaked to the skin!"

Abe obeyed quickly. His stepmother was right. His feet felt like chunks of ice. He pulled the blanket around him and hugged the shivering dog.

"You had better give up rabbit hunting for a while," he said to the little dog. "I wouldn't like to do that again soon!"

The dog whined and looked up at him. Then he yapped once as if in agreement and curled up next to Abe.

A Ticket to the Circus

Milly Howard and Rebecca Fitchner

illustrated by Paula Cheadle

How would you like to be the shortest nine-year-old boy around? Richy certainly doesn't. But when the circus comes to town, he learns that being short has its advantages after all!

The News

It was Richy's job to tend the family garden, so he had been pulling weeds all afternoon. He had weeded everything except the tomatoes when his mother called him to the house. She met him on the back porch with a glass of lemonade in one hand and a nickel in the other. "I've been mending a pair of your father's socks and have run out of darning floss. Esther is napping, and supper is on the stove, so I need you to run to the general store for me. It closes early on Saturday, so you'll have to hurry."

Richy disappeared around the side of the house. With the speed and accuracy that come with practice, Richy hurdled a peony bush and did cartwheels all the way to the shed. He rolled out his bike and raced off down the street to the general store.

He took the steps up to the store two at a time, swung the screen door open, and stopped. Never had he seen so many people at one time! No one seemed to be shopping. Everyone was just milling about, chattering excitedly. Richy found his way to the counter and stood there patiently, but no one noticed him, not even the clerk behind the counter.

"Pardon me, sir," Richy began, "but I've come to buy some darning floss for my mother."

The clerk continued talking to someone else. Richy cleared his throat quite loudly. Still no response. Richy flinched at the thought, but he knew he would have to ring the little counter bell if he were to make his purchase before closing time. Ding! The clerk glanced from side to side with a puzzled expression on his face.

"Down here, sir," said Richy sheepishly.

"Ah, yes, Richy, didn't see you there. And what'll it be today?"

"Some darning floss for my mother, please."

"All righty. That'll be three cents, please."

Richy paid the man and asked, "What's all the excitement about?"

"Haven't you heard? The circus is coming to town!"

"The circus! When?"

"Next month. August 10 to be exact. I'm surprised you haven't seen the posters. Some men from the circus were in town this afternoon putting them up."

Richy thanked the man for his help, stuffed the darning floss and change into his pocket, and raced outside. Everywhere he looked there were huge, colorful posters describing the many wonders of the circus and proclaiming Friday, August 10, 1928, as the date of the show. Richy fairly flew home with the good news!

He sped up the driveway yelling, "The circus is coming!"

Little Esther caught the circus spirit right away and marched around the house tooting an imaginary horn. Mother began counting the money in the cookie jar.

Richy tossed in the two pennies from his pocket and handed his mother the darning floss.

"Mother, can we afford to take the whole family?"

"Not yet, Richy," Mother sighed. "But we'll just save every penny we can and keep darning our socks instead of buying new ones!"

"And I'll sell some fresh vegetables from the garden!" added Richy. He ran outside to finish weeding the tomatoes.

Father came out to the garden as soon as he got home from work. "The garden looks mighty fine, Son."

"Thank you, Father."

"By the way, Thomas Betchler stopped by the lumberyard this afternoon. He's with the Betchler Brothers Circus. He said they were looking for strong boys to help set up the circus next month. He also said each boy who helped would get a free pass to the circus. I told them there was a boy at my house that they could count on."

Richy let out a hoot, hugged his father, and did a one-handed flip right there next to the tomatoes.

Getting Ready

The entire town was looking forward to the coming of the circus. The children had nearly memorized the circus posters. The boys especially liked the lunging tiger with its white fangs and fiery eyes. All the girls were dazzled by the pure white horses.

Richy's family was busy finding ways to earn extra money for their circus fund. Mother contributed what she was paid to sew a dress for the lady next door. Father put in the twenty-five-cent tip he got for making a lumber delivery after hours. Even little Esther gave the penny she earned helping Widow Johnson wash windows.

Richy was counting on selling tomatoes to make his donation to the cookie jar. When the first tomatoes ripened in the warmth of August, he had no trouble selling them, because they were beauties.

In fact, sales were so good that when Richy added his money to the circus fund, there was enough to take Widow Johnson with them. Now August 10 couldn't come soon enough!

Several men from the circus came a day early to make sure everything would be ready for the circus when it arrived. They set up camp at the edge of town in the clearing where the circus would be held and began their work. They bought food and supplies from the general store and hauled wagonload after wagonload of hay and feed from the mill.

Richy and the other boys watched from afar. Their help was not needed until the next day.

Richy was part of the crowd that met the main circus train when it pulled in at six o'clock the next morning. From the limb of a nearby tree, Richy watched the unloading begin.

First, steel plates were placed between the railroad cars to form one long bridge. Then teams of horses pulled the circus wagons across the bridge and down a ramp to the ground. It was hard to tell what was in

each wagon except for those with "WILD ANIMALS—
DANGER—DO NOT TOUCH!" painted on their
canvas covers. Richy joined the children who followed
the wagons to the clearing at the edge of town.

The smell of bacon and eggs greeted the hungry
circus company, but breakfast was eaten quickly, and
the business of setting up the Betchler Brothers Circus
began. The stake-driving crews picked up their
sledgehammers and went right to work. With the
combined power of several elephants and dozens of
men, the three main poles for the big top were raised.
Richy and the other boys helped to unroll and lace
together the pieces of tent canvas. The elephants and
men raised the huge tent roof and set the medium-
sized poles in place. The tent ropes were tightened,
making the tent look like a great flat saucer. At last
the big top was ready for the seats to be set up inside.

The boys helped raise the sideshow and menagerie tents. Then they were divided into two groups. One group helped feed the horses and elephants, and Richy's group carried buckets of water to the circus performers. Richy's group leader took one look at him and shook his head. "I'm afraid this bucket is too heavy for a little fellow like you. I'll have to take it to the Arabian Princess myself."

"But, sir—" Richy began, but the man was already walking away. Richy's face got hot, and he felt a lump in his throat.

The man turned back. "Hey, kid, there is something you could do to help. Take this letter to Lou Weaver. He's in the first wagon past the cook house."

Letter in hand, Richy started walking slowly toward the cook house. He tried to swallow the lump

in his throat. Richy was still in low spirits when he knocked at the door of Lou Weaver's wagon.

"Come in."

Richy opened the door and saw a man sitting behind a large desk. "I have a letter for Lou Weaver."

"That's me. Dr. Louis J. Weaver, the circus crowd-pleaser!" He took the letter and began opening it.

"Are you a clown, Mr. Weaver?"

"I am indeed! But please call me Lou. And who, pray tell, are you?"

"My name is Richy. I'm one of the boys helping set up the circus today. Well, I *was* helping set up until . . ." Richy hesitated. That lump was back in his throat.

"Until what?" Lou asked, setting his letter aside. "You can tell me."

So Richy poured out the whole story.

"I understand your problem much better than you may think," said Lou, slipping out from behind his desk. Richy was surprised to find himself looking at Lou eye to eye.

"Yes, Richy, I'm a midget. But there's nothing I can do to change that, so I just do my best with what I have. And do you know what? I've discovered that there are a lot of things I can do that other folks can't. How many people do you know who can do a one-handed flip?"

"I don't know of anyone but myself."

"So you're an acrobat, Richy! That's wonderful! Why don't you show me a few of your tricks, and I'll show you some of mine." So off they went, and what a grand time they had! Lou taught Richy several new acrobatic stunts. He even taught Richy how to ride a unicycle, which was Lou's big solo act in the circus. They didn't realize how late it was getting until another clown stopped by to remind Lou of their meeting in five minutes. Lou had to rush off to his meeting, and Richy needed to pick up his free pass and hurry home.

Richy got to the ticket
wagon just as the last few boys
were picking up their passes.
Richy got in line behind them,
and when it was his turn, the
ticket man didn't see him.
Down went the little window
on the ticket wagon, and Richy
was left standing there without
his pass to the circus!

The New Clown

When he got home, Richy couldn't bring himself to tell his family what had happened. That evening he got ready to go to the circus as if nothing were wrong and then asked if he might go early. Father winked at Mother and said, "Yes."

Richy got to the edge of town and headed straight for the ticket wagon. He stood on his toes and spoke as loudly as he could, "Sir, I'm one of the boys who helped set up the circus today. I didn't get my free pass this afternoon, so I'd like to pick it up now, if I may."

"You may not! What proof do I have that they actually put a wee fellow like you to work?"

"You have my word, sir."

"That isn't enough. I need the word of your group leader. Find him and you'll have your free pass. Next."

Richy moved aside for the next person in line and then stood frozen in his tracks. He didn't know where to start looking. He didn't even know the name of his group leader. There was only one person he knew to ask, so Richy made a beeline for the first wagon past

the cook house. Richy was relieved to see a light on inside. He knocked and called out, "Lou, it's Richy. May I come in?"

"Sure, pal. The door's open."

Richy opened the door and saw Lou sitting at his desk.

"Richy, why aren't you with your family?"

Richy told Lou about not getting his free pass.

"He couldn't see me," Richy said. "And that man out there doesn't think I deserve to get into the circus. I guess I'm not much good for anything."

"Well, now," Lou said. He scratched his chin thoughtfully. "You're a pretty fine acrobat."

Richy rolled his eyes. "Yeah, but . . ."

"And you know how to ride a unicycle, and you're not too tall," Lou said.

"But none of that counts for anything," Richy said.

"Sounds like all the right things to get you into the circus. That *is* what you're trying to do, isn't it?"

"Yes, but . . ." Richy didn't understand.

"Hold on. I'll be back in a minute." Lou jumped from his chair and ran for the door.

Soon he returned with a triumphant look. "I want you to do my show with me tonight," he said.

"Me?" Richy couldn't believe it.

Lou smiled at him. "We did practice together today. Well, what are you waiting for? You need to get ready for the show!"

Richy let out a hoot and did a one-handed flip right there in Lou's wagon.

Lou seated Richy at his dressing table and applied the clown makeup with quick, sure strokes. Richy laughed as a frizzy red wig went on next. Then Lou reached in his trunk and pulled out a costume with bright polka dots and a matching hat. "Here. Put these on."

Richy dressed, taking care not to smear his new face, and stood before the mirror, unbelieving. Just as he finished, the circus band began to play its first song.

"Ah! Perfect timing!" Lou said. "Follow me."

Lou gave Richy last-minute instructions as they walked to the big top. "After the lion tamer is through, there will be a drum roll, and the ringmaster will say, 'And now, ladies and gentlemen, Richy the Great, riding his one-wheeled wonder!' That's when you enter and ride around the hippodrome just as I showed you this afternoon. I'll be turning somersaults behind you."

At the big top a circus worker stood waiting for them, steadying Lou's unicycle.

"Richy, this friend of mine will take you from here. I'll be right behind you. Go ahead. You're in— more than any of those boys with their free passes!"

Richy turned toward the big top. As he heard the music begin and the ringmaster's voice, he suddenly felt a little taller.

The Beast of the Desert

Milly Howard

*illustrated by Del Thompson
and Sam Laterza*

Wild Horse Canyon

Leather creaked as Orly shifted in his saddle. One of the ranch hands turned to look at him.

"Tired?" Slim asked, grinning at Orly. "When I was your age, I could ride fifty miles without getting off my horse. Why, one time . . ."

Orly grinned as Slim launched into one of his tall tales. Tired? On his first wild horse roundup? Orly thought of all the times he had begged to come and had been told that he was not old enough. He straightened in his saddle, easing the growing stiffness in his legs.

The men had been riding since before dawn. Last week a rancher had told Grandpa that a red stallion had been seen in the canyons bordering the desert. They had never gone this far on a roundup before, but Grandpa said that this particular stallion and his band of mares were worth riding miles for.

288

The red-rimmed canyons ahead of them were outlined against the bright sun, their rocky walls glowing pink and orange. The men slowed their horses, looking for signs of the wild horses. Seeing none, they rode into the canyons. Orly craned his neck, staring up at the rocks towering above him, almost forgetting about the wild horses.

Grandpa turned down another canyon, holding his hand up for quiet. Orly held his breath but heard nothing. When Grandpa motioned, they rode on and entered an arroyo.

"A stream! and grass!" Orly said, surprised.

"This is why the stallion is bringing his mares here," Grandpa said. He inspected the rocky walls carefully. "Here," he said, pointing to an opening in the rocks. "A dry wash."

Orly gave a questioning look. Grandpa said, "Used to be part of the stream. It's dried up now. We can block it off, drive the horses into it, and capture the whole band."

He turned to Slim. "Slim, climb up on those rocks and keep an eye out for the stallion and his mares."

"Grandpa, may I . . ." Orly began.

Grandpa grinned. "Can you use some help, Slim?"

"Why, sure," Slim replied. "Got another story to tell, anyway."

Orly followed Slim, matching handholds up the rocks. At the top they lay on a huge flat rock, looking out over the desert.

Slim had almost finished his tale when a trail of dust appeared on the horizon.

"Here they come!" Slim pushed his hat back on his head and grinned at Orly. "I can't wait to get my saddle on that red stallion. What a ride we'll have!"

Orly peered over the edge of the rock and shaded his eyes against the glare of the sun. "Aw, you can't see that far, Slim," he said.

"Why, you had better believe I can, Son. Just wait and see."

Orly watched the
trail of dust drift
skyward as it
moved closer. At last
he could see the band of wild
horses, manes flowing
as they galloped
toward the
arroyo.

"Let's get moving," said Slim. Orly backed away
from the edge of the rock, and they scrambled down.

"The horses are coming, Grandpa!" Orly called.
"Are you ready?"

Grandpa looked up from the tangle of mesquite
branches he and the cowboys had used to block the
dry wash. He shoved the last branch into place and
wiped his face.

"About as ready as we'll ever be," he said to the
excited boy. "Mount up, partner!"

"Hurry, Grandpa. They might leave before we get
there!" Orly urged.

"Hold on there, Orly," laughed Grandpa. "That red
stallion brought his mares down for water and grass.
They're in no hurry to leave."

As he and Orly swung into their saddles, Grandpa called to the cowboys.

"Make sure you get the horses turned into the dry wash. That stallion is a smart one. He won't give us another chance."

"Sure thing, Mr. Sloan," Slim said, laughing. "The animal that can outsmart Old Slim here hasn't been born!"

Orly and Grandpa rode their horses around to the mouth of the arroyo. The band of horses had finished drinking and were grazing along the stream.

"Beautiful, aren't they?" Grandpa pointed to the leader of the band. The stallion's red coat was easy to spot among the darker mares. "He's the one we need to head off. The others will follow him.

"Let's go, Son," said Grandpa. They spurred their horses out from under the trees. Yelling and waving their hats, they rode toward the band of horses.

The red stallion reared and galloped away, his mares close behind him. They splashed through the shallow water and raced toward the dry wash.

"Hi-ee!" yelled Orly, waving his hat in the air. Through the dust he saw Slim and the others gallop out in front of the racing horses. Then he saw another dim shape appear behind the waving men. A roar from the strange creature echoed in the canyon.

As Slim turned to look behind him, the wild horses swung into the dry wash. They skidded to a halt at the blocked end. Then with a wild rush, the stallion headed back through the opening.

"Stop them, boys!" shouted Grandpa. He and Orly urged their horses faster, trying to close the gap.

But the cowboys were having trouble. Their horses were jumping and bucking, trying to get away from a large animal.

Grandpa swung his horse around, pushing Orly's pony out of the way as the wild horses swept past them. Orly's eyes filled with tears as the horses disappeared around the bend.

"We've lost them, Grandpa," he cried.

Grandpa didn't answer. He was staring at the huge, dirty beast trotting through the dust. It had

long, thin legs and a curved
neck. It held its head high
and looked down its
long nose at them.

Slim galloped up,
swinging his rope. "Let's
see what this thing is," he
said. The rope looped
neatly over the
strange animal's neck.

The animal jerked
its head back and spat.
Slim dropped the
rope and wiped his
wet face.

"Dirty beast!" Slim scrubbed and scrubbed his face.
The animal turned and trotted away into the dry wash.

"Throw those mesquite branches across the gap,"
Slim called to the other cowboys. The animal moved
slowly about as they blocked the way out of the
makeshift corral.

"What is it, Grandpa?" asked Orly.

"Well, Orly," replied Grandpa, "I think it's a camel."

"A camel!"

The Broncobuster

Orly climbed on the rocks to get a better look at the camel.

"It does have a hump, Grandpa. But where did it come from?"

Grandpa rubbed his chin. "The army brought some camels to America about fifteen years ago. They were going to use them in the desert. Nothing ever came of it, though."

Slim stuffed his handkerchief back into his pocket. "Didn't they just turn them loose in the desert when the Civil War started?"

"That's what I heard," Grandpa replied, "though some were used in traveling animal acts. This one probably hasn't been loose too long. It's not very scared of us."

One of the cowboys looked sideways at Slim. "That's one four-legged beast you can't ride," he said slyly.

"Slim can ride anything! You can ride him, can't you, Slim?" asked Orly.

"Why, sure, Orly," Slim said. "It's a four-legged animal like any other one. Too bad we don't have a saddle to fit him."

296

"Slim, you've been bragging that you can ride anything big enough to hold you, saddle or bareback," said the cowboy. "This one's big enough to hold you all right."

The cowboy jumped down and grabbed the end of the rope. "Here you go," he said, tossing it to Slim.

"Ride him, Slim!" called Orly.

Slim climbed down into the dry wash. "How do I get on?" he asked.

"Lead him over to that big rock," said Grandpa. "You can try jumping on him."

Slim didn't look too happy, but he climbed on the rock and pulled on the rope. When the camel was close enough, Slim took a deep breath and jumped.

The camel stepped sideways, and Slim sprawled flat in the dust. The men roared with laughter and slapped their legs.

Slim staggered to his feet and looked at the camel. The camel stared back at Slim.

"I'm not through with you yet," Slim said, climbing back on the rock.

"Wait a minute, Slim," called Grandpa. "Put this through the hole in his nose."

He tossed Slim a long piece of leather. When Slim looped it through the camel's nose, he was able to pull the camel closer to him. Again he jumped. This time he landed on the camel's hump. For a moment it looked as though he had made it. Then he slid slowly over the other side. It was seven feet to the ground. Slim hit hard. For a moment he lay quietly. Then he crawled to his feet and brushed himself off.

His critics shouted encouraging remarks that Slim stubbornly ignored.

"Grandpa," said Orly, "the stories in my schoolbooks say camels always kneel to let the riders get on. Can we pull him down for Slim?"

"Good idea, Son," said Grandpa. He climbed over the rocks. Two of the other cowboys jumped down into the corral. Together they pulled the protesting camel to its knees.

"Hop on, Slim," the cowboys shouted. Slim climbed on the camel's hump. Clutching the leather strap in one hand and holding on with his knees, he waved his hat and said, "Let's go!"

In one swift movement, the camel unfolded its long back legs. Slim flew over the camel's head.

"Good ride, Slim!" The men slapped each other on the back.

"This is no picnic, you know," Slim said as he crawled to his feet. "I'd like to see you try it!" He shook his hair out of his eyes and glared at the long-legged beast. "Pull him down," he said.

The men brought the camel to its knees again. Slim climbed back on the hump. This time he pulled the strap tight with both hands and braced his feet on either side of the camel.

"Let's go!" he yelled again.

This time when the camel lurched to its back feet, Slim braced himself against the camel's long neck. Then the camel unfolded its front legs and stood up. Slim clung tightly to the strap, swaying with the movement of the camel.

"He did it!" yelled Orly.

The men cheered.

Slim grinned from ear to ear. "It's all in knowing how," he said.

"Can we take it home, Grandpa?" Orly asked.

"Well, it sure isn't what we came for," said Grandpa. "There's not a chance of catching the wild horses now. But won't the folks be surprised." He chuckled at the thought. "Can you ride it home, Slim?"

Slim swayed back and forth as he rode the camel around the corral. "Sure can, Mr. Sloan."

It was a strange crew riding through the canyons on the way home. Slim rode far ahead of the still nervous horses. As the camel topped the crest of the hill, it was outlined against the setting sun.

"Look, Grandpa!" said Orly. He pointed to the camel and its rider.

Grandpa shook his head. "Who would have thought of it? A camel in America!"

Mission over Mexico

(A true story)

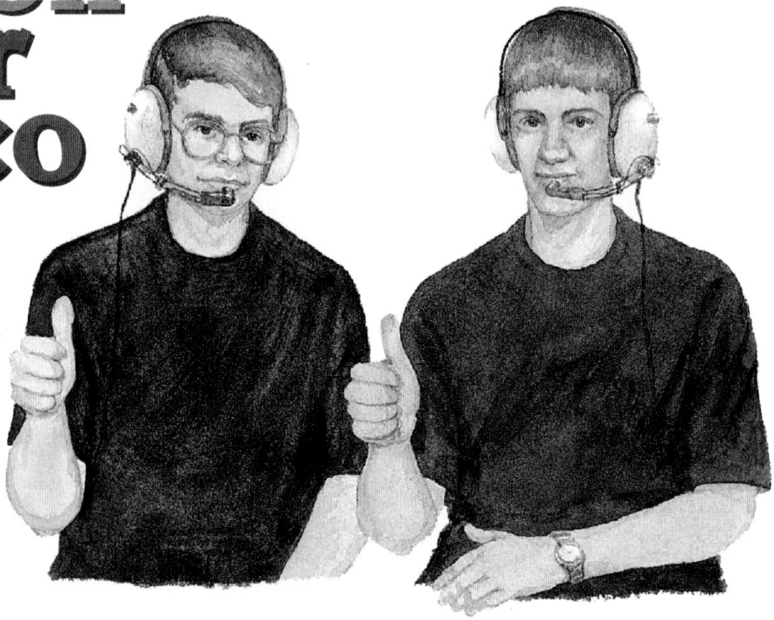

Susan W. Young

illustrated by
Mary Ann Lumm

Mission Begun

John Pruden climbed into the C210. "It's a fine day for flying." He adjusted his headset and flipped on the radio.

"Sure is." Mike Poindexter pulled his mouthpiece forward. "Are we all set?"

"All set and ready for takeoff." Mr. Pruden glanced over his shoulder at the back seat. "How about you guys back there? All set?"

"Sure are, Mr. Pruden." Jason and Matt spoke at the same time. They looked at each other and then gave him a thumbs up.

Mr. Pruden eased onto the runway and waited for the "all clear" on the radio. When he got it he taxied down, gave it some throttle, and the small plane lifted into the air. "Novillero, here we come."

"I'm glad you could come down and make this trip with me, John. The missionaries on the island of Novillero need our help." Mr. Poindexter checked their location.

"Do they know we're coming?" Mr. Pruden scanned the clear blue sky. "We should make good time. There's nothing in our way to slow us down."

Mr. Poindexter checked the map. "I couldn't let them know we were coming because there are no phones or radios on the island. So as soon as we find the airport, we'll fly low over the missionary's house to signal him. Then we'll fly back to the airport. He'll drive over to pick us up."

Jason's voice came over the headset. "There are no phones or radios, but there's an airport?"

Mr. Poindexter laughed. "It's only a dirt strip with no buildings, no electricity, and no running water."

"Does anyone man this airport?" Matt asked.

"About twelve soldiers are stationed there for three weeks at a time. They sleep in tents and make sure no one uses the airport to fly in illegal drugs." Mr. Poindexter pointed to the left. "Look, there it is now."

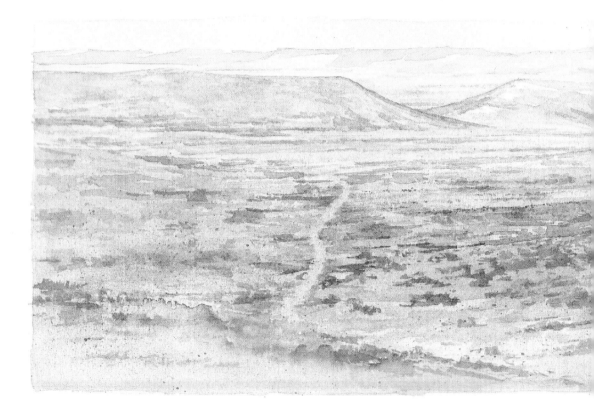

Mr. Pruden tipped the wings to take a look. The dirt airstrip stretched through the trees like a brown shoelace. Mr. Poindexter had described it perfectly. Nothing else was down there.

"I'll enter these coordinates so that we can find the airport on the way back." Mr. Poindexter looked down to check the map. "Go ahead and head west toward the missionary's house."

Mr. Pruden checked the altitude. They were flying at about 4,000 feet. He checked the other gauges. Everything looked great.

Mission Interrupted

Suddenly a huge bird appeared to Mr. Pruden's left, falling straight toward them.

"Look out! It's coming right through the windshield." John gripped the controls.

The bird disappeared, but a second later there was a loud thud. The plane began to jerk up and down like a roller coaster.

"We're going down!" Jason shouted.

"What happened?" Matt yelled into the headset.

Mr. Pruden struggled to control the plane. The roller coaster movement slowed, but the plane began pulling to the left. He pushed his foot against the right rudder pedal as hard as he could.

"Which pedal are you pushing?" Mr. Poindexter shouted in his ear. Mr. Pruden felt Mr. Poindexter's foot push against his.

"I'm giving it full right rudder," he shouted back. "But it's no use. We're veering to the left and losing altitude. We're not going to make it without God's help."

Mr. Poindexter began to pray aloud. "Lord, help us. You can control this plane. Please help us."

Mr. Pruden felt a great calmness come over him. His mind cleared. The plane steadied, but it was still pulling left. "We have to get to level ground," he said. "I don't know how much longer I can hold her."

"Head for the airport. It's all swamp below." Mr. Poindexter looked out the window. "Swamp and alligators. Turn back to the airport."

Mr. Pruden struggled to turn the plane in the direction of the airport. "Jason," he said into his mouthpiece, "can you see what the damage is?"

There was no answer.

"Did you hear me, Jason? What's the damage look like?"

Mr. Poindexter looked back at the boys. "I don't know what he saw, John, but it must be bad. He's as white as a sheet."

"What about you, Matt? Can you see what happened?" Mr. Pruden fought to keep the plane from corkscrewing to the ground.

"I can't see much, but it looks like we've got a hole in the left horizontal stabilizer." Matt's voice was shaking. "That's all I can see from here."

Mr. Poindexter began to pray out loud again.

Mr. Pruden prayed silently. "Lord, You have to help me control this plane. Help me get us on the ground." He wiped the sweat from his brow. "All right everybody, tighten your seatbelts. With God's help we're going to get this plane on the ground."

There was not a sound from the back. Mr. Pruden knew the boys were praying.

Mr. Pruden checked the gauges. The plane was dropping at a rate of 1,200 feet per minute. He gave it more throttle.

The engine sputtered. It sputtered and stopped.

"Now what?" Mr. Poindexter leaned forward to look at the fuel gauge. "We can't be out of fuel."

"You're right. We've got fuel, but it must not be reaching the intake valves. The force of this slide is pushing it to the outside of the tank, away from the valves."

"Is there any fuel left in the other tank?" Mr. Poindexter reached toward the switch.

"Only about seven gallons. We won't go far on that."

"But at least we'll go." Mr. Poindexter flipped the switch.

The engine roared. Mr. Pruden gave it full throttle.

"What are you doing?" Mr. Poindexter shouted. "You'll ruin the engine running it at full speed."

"It's the only way. If I don't keep up the speed, I'll lose control of the plane. Besides, we're still dropping. We've got to get to the airport fast."

Mr. Poindexter looked at his watch and then at the map. "We're only ten minutes away. We can make it."

No one said another word until the narrow dirt strip appeared below them.

"There it is!" Mr. Poindexter shouted.

"Don't stop praying. I still have to get her on the ground." Mr. Pruden pitched the nose of the plane down so that he could see the runway clearly.

"Do you want flaps?" Mr. Poindexter had his hand ready.

"Yes, but just a little. Too much and it'll stall the plane."

When there was only two hundred feet to go, Mr. Pruden dropped the landing gear. The drag of the landing gear pulled them straight down at full power. Slowly he shut down the power. Ten feet above the runway the engine quit. The plane dropped to the runway and rolled to a stop.

"Everyone all right?" Mr. Pruden opened the door and stepped out onto the airstrip. He walked to the back of the plane. The broken stabilizer hung from shards of broken metal. The remains of the huge sea bird covered the jagged pieces. Mr. Pruden's knees went out from under him, and he knelt in the sand. "Thank you, Lord. Thank you for a miracle."

Mission Accomplished

Twelve soldiers walked across the airstrip. Their uniforms were dusty. Rifles hung over their shoulders.

"*Hola.*" The face of the lieutenant was stern and unsmiling.

"*Hola,*" Mr. Poindexter replied in Spanish.

Mike explained what had happened. The lieutenant listened. Then he began to ask questions.

"He needs to see our papers." Mr. Poindexter motioned for Mr. Pruden to get them. "Don't worry. It's just routine."

The lieutenant checked them. He returned them to Mr. Poindexter.

"He says we're free to go. We can leave the plane here," Mr. Poindexter said to Mr. Pruden. "I guess we'll have to walk out to the road and catch a ride to the nearest town."

The four of them began to tie down the plane. Most of the soldiers had drifted away. One of them came nearer.

"This looks very bad." He examined the broken part. "You are lucky to live. You should all be dead."

Mr. Poindexter stood up. "You're right. We should be dead. But we are alive not because we are lucky. We are alive because it was God's plan. God saved my life today so that I could tell you about Jesus Christ and what He has done for you."

Five more of the soldiers moved closer. The first soldier motioned for them to stop. He pointed to the plane and spoke to them in Spanish.

"We want to hear what you have to tell us. We want to know why you are still alive."

Mr. Poindexter cleared his throat. "We are standing here right now because God saved our lives. When our plane was hit, we thought it would crash. We thought we were going to die. But we were ready to die. We were ready to meet God. But God wanted us to live so that we could come here to tell you how much He loves you. Jesus died to save you. Jesus died so that you could live."

The six soldiers listened carefully as Mr. Poindexter told them over and over that God had saved him from death so that he could tell them how to have eternal life. Then he was finished.

One by one the six men knelt beside the plane and asked God to save them from their sins. Mr. Pruden, Jason, and Matt knelt with them and thanked God for another miracle.

"We thank you for the message you have brought." The first soldier shook Mr. Poindexter's hand. "We will guard your plane until you return. We will make sure it is safe."

Mr. Pruden, Jason, and Matt gave the men copies of the Gospel of John and Romans.

"When we return for the plane, we'll bring you each a Bible," Mr. Poindexter told the men. "Until then, read these. They are God's Word." The soldiers shook hands with each of the men and returned to their tents.

"Today we have seen two miracles." Mr. Pruden put his hand on Mike's shoulder. "We were saved from death to life so that those men could be saved from eternal death to eternal life."

Glossary

This glossary has information about selected words found in this reader. You can find meanings of words as they are used in the stories. Certain unusual words such as foreign names are included so that you can pronounce them correctly when you read.

The pronunciation symbols below show how to pronounce each vowel and several of the less familiar consonants.

ă	pat	ĕ	pet	îr	fierce
ā	pay	ē	be	ŏ	pot
âr	care	ĭ	pit	ō	go
ä	father	ī	pie	ô	paw, for, ball

oi	oil	ŭ	cut	zh	vision
o͝o	book	ûr	fur	ə	ago, item,
o͞o	boot	*th*	the		pencil, atom,
yo͞o	abuse	th	thin		circus
ou	out	hw	which	ər	butter

a•bode | ə bōd´ | —*verb* Stayed or remained in the same place.

ac•com•plish | ə kŏm´plĭsh | —*verb* To finish after setting out to do; achieve; complete.

ac•cu•ra•cy | ăk´yər ə sē | —*noun* The condition of being correct and exact.

ac•ro•bat | ăk´rə băt | —*noun* A person who is skilled in performing on a trapeze, walking on a tightrope, and tumbling.

acrobat

ad•just | ə jŭst´ | —*verb* 1. To change in order to make right or better. 2. To move into a different position.

air•craft car•ri•er | âr´krăft kăr´ē ər | —*noun* A large ship that is part of a navy and is used as an air base.

aircraft carrier

ar•roy•o | ə roi´ō | —*noun* A deep gully cut out by a stream that comes and goes with the rains; dry gulch.

bard | bärd | —*noun* A singing poet who composes and recites verse about history and legends.

bar•ley | bär´lē | —*noun* A plant that is like grass and bears seeds. Barley is used as food.

barley

318

bee•line | bē´līn | —*noun* A direct, straight course.

big top | bĭg tŏp | —*noun* The main tent of a circus.

brace | brās | —*verb* To support or strengthen.

budge | bŭj | —*verb* To move or cause to move slightly.

can•vas | kăn´vəs | —*noun* A heavy, coarse cloth used for making tents, sails, and so on.

cap•i•tal | kăp´ĭ tl | —*noun* A city where the government of a state or country is located.

cap•i•tol | kăp´ĭ tl | —*noun* The building in which a state legislature meets.

car•riage | kâr´ĭj | —*noun* A passenger vehicle that has four wheels and is usually pulled by horses.

carriage

cease | sēs | —*verb* To bring or come to an end; stop.

chant•er | chăn´tər | —*noun* The pipe of a bagpipe on which the melody is played.

chron•i•cle | krŏn´ĭ kəl | —*noun* A chronological record of historical events.

chanter

ă	pat	ĕ	pet
ā	pay	ē	be
âr	care	ĭ	pit
ä	father	ī	pie

îr	fierce	oi	oil
ŏ	pot	o͝o	book
ō	go	o͞o	boot
ô	paw,	yo͞o	abuse
	for	ou	out

ŭ	cut	ə	ago,
ûr	fur		item,
th	the		pencil,
th	thin		atom,
hw	which		circus
zh	vision	ər	butter

colo•nel | kûr′nəl | —*noun* An officer in the army, air force, or marine corps. A colonel ranks above a major and below a general.

corral

con•gre•ga•tion | kŏng′grə gā′shən | —*noun* A group of people gathered for religious worship.

co•or•di•nate | kō ôr′dn āt′ | —*noun* A number or one of a set of numbers and letters used to locate a place on a map.

coyote

cork•screw | kôrk′skrōō | —*verb* To move in a spiral or twisting manner.

cor•ral | kə răl′ | —*noun* A pen or place with a fence for keeping cattle or horses.

court•yard | kôrt′yärd | or | kōrt′yärd | —*noun* An open space surrounded by walls or buildings.

coy•o•te | kī ō′tē | or | kī′ōt | —*noun* A North American animal that looks somewhat like a wolf. Coyotes are common in the western part of the United States and Canada.

darning floss

cu•ri•ous | kyŏŏr′ē əs | —*adjective* Eager to learn or know.

D **darn•ing floss** | därn′ĭng flôs | —*noun* A soft, loosely twisted thread used to mend a hole in clothing.

ă pat	ĕ pet	îr fierce	oi oil	ŭ cut	ə ago,
ā pay	ē be	ŏ pot	ōō book	ûr fur	item,
âr care	ĭ pit	ō go	ōō boot	th the	pencil,
ä father	ī pie	ô paw,	yōō abuse	th thin	atom,
		for	ou out	hw which	circus
				zh vision	ər butter

de•cree | dĭ **crē´** | —*noun* An official order; a law.

des•ert | **dĕz´** ərt | —*noun* A very dry region covered with sand or pebbles. Few things grow in a desert.

de•sert | dĭ **zûrt´** | —*verb* To leave or abandon.

din | dĭn | —*noun* Loud, confusing noise.

dis•tress | dĭ **strĕs´** | —*noun* Serious danger or trouble.

dry wash

drawl | drôl | —*verb* To speak slowly.

drone | drōn | —*verb* To talk in a boring, dull way.

drum•roll | **drŭm´** rōl | —*noun* To beat a drum in a continuous series of very short blows.

dry wash | drī wŏsh | —*noun* The dry bed of a stream.

E **eb•on•y** | **eb´** ə nē | —*noun* The hard, black wood of a tree that grows in the tropics.

el•e•va•tor | **el´** ə **vā´** tər | —*noun* A platform or small room that can be raised or lowered to carry people from one level to another in a building.

ebony

etch | ĕch | —*verb* To cut lines into a surface.

e•ter•nal | ĭ **tûr´** nəl | —*adjective* Lasting forever.

F

fire pan | fīr păn | —*noun* A container to hold the fire in a hot-air balloon.

flinch | flĭnch | —*verb* To pull back quickly in pain or fear; wince.

flur•ry | flûr´ē | —*noun* A sudden outburst; a stir.

fringe

fringe | frĭnj | —*noun* An edge made of hanging threads or cords.

G

gal•lows | găl´ōz | —*noun* A frame from which criminals are hanged. The typical gallows is made of two upright posts with a beam across them. A noose is tied to the beam.

gauge | gāj | —*noun* A measuring instrument.

glint | glĭnt | —*noun* A momentary flash of light; a sparkle.

gopher

go•pher | gō´fər | —*noun* A small North American animal that has pouches like pockets in its cheeks. Gophers live in burrows that they dig in the ground.

guf•faw | gə fô´ | —*noun* A loud or rude burst of laughter.

H   **halt** | hôlt | —*noun* A stop; a pause.

ă	pat	ĕ	pet	îr	fierce	oi	oil	ŭ	cut	ə	ago,
ā	pay	ē	be	ŏ	pot	o͝o	book	ûr	fur		item,
âr	care	ĭ	pit	ō	go	o͞o	boot	th	the		pencil,
ä	father	ī	pie	ô	paw,	yo͞o	abuse	th	thin		atom,
					for	ou	out	hw	which		circus
								zh	vision	ər	butter

har•ness | här´nĭs | —*noun* Gear used by astronauts to keep them safe during liftoff and in free fall.

harp•si•chord | härp´sĭ kôrd´ | —*noun* A keyboard instrument similar to the piano. A harpsichord's strings are plucked by quills or picks rather than being struck by little hammers.

harpsichord

head•wa•ters | hĕd´wŏ tərs | —*noun* The water from which a river rises or begins.

hearth | härth | —*noun* The floor of a fireplace and the area around it.

hip•po•drome | hĭp´ə drōm | —*noun* An oval track made especially for horses.

hor•i•zon•tal | hôr´ĭ zŏn´tl | —*adjective* Parallel to the ground; straight across.

hearth

hus•tle | hŭs´əl | —*verb* To hurry; rush.

hy•dro•gen | hī´drə jən | —*noun* A gas that is very light and that burns easily. Hydrogen is one of the chemical elements.

I **il•le•gal** | ĭ lē´gəl | —*adjective* Against the law or against the rules.

hippodrome

i•vo•ry | ī´və rē | —*noun* The smooth, hard, yellowish white material that forms the tusks of elephants and certain other animals.

J

jester

jes•ter | jĕs´tər | —*noun* In the Middle Ages, a person kept by kings, queens, and other nobles to entertain or amuse them.

K

kilt | kĭlt | —*noun* A pleated, plaid skirt that reaches down to the knees. Kilts are worn by men in Scotland.

knight | nīt | —*noun* A soldier in the Middle Ages who served and pledged loyalty to a king or lord.

L

kilt

land•scape | lănd´skāp | —*noun* A piece of land or countryside that has its own special appearance.

land•slide | lănd´slīd | —*noun* The sliding down a hill or mountain of a large amount of earth and rock.

lank•y | lăng´kē | —*adjective* Tall, thin, and clumsy.

lar•i•at | lăr´ē ĭt | —*noun* A long rope with a sliding noose at one end, used especially to catch horses or cattle; lasso.

lariat

Lat•in | lăt´n | —*noun* The language of ancient Romans.

lo•cust | lō´kəst | —*noun* A kind of grasshopper that travels in huge swarms. Locusts often do great damage to growing crops.

lute | lo͞ot | —*noun* A stringed musical instrument with a body shaped like half a pear and with a long, bent neck. It is played by plucking the strings.

lute

M

ma•jor | mā´ jər | —*noun* An officer in the army, air force, or marine corps who ranks above a captain.

me•nag•er•ie | mə năj´ ə rē | —*noun* A collection of live wild animals on exhibition.

mes•quite | mĕ **skēt´** | or | **mĕs´** kēt | —*noun* A thorny shrub or tree of southwestern North America. It has feathery leaves and long, narrow pods.

mesquite

me•zu•zah | mə zo͞oz´ ə | —*noun* A small piece of paper with the verses from Deuteronomy 6:4-9 and 11:13-21 written on it and marked with the word *Shaddai,* a name of the Almighty. It is rolled up in a small box and nailed to the door frame of a home as a sign that a Jewish family lives there.

mim•ic | **mĭm´** ĭk | —*verb* To copy; imitate.

mir•a•cle | **mĭr´** ə kəl | —*noun* An amazing or unlikely person, thing, or feat; a wonder.

mezuzah

mourn | môrn | —*verb* To feel or show sorrow or grief for a death or loss.

ă pat	ĕ pet	îr fierce	oi oil	ŭ cut	ə ago,
ā pay	ē be	ŏ pot	o͝o book	ûr fur	item,
âr care	ĭ pit	ō go	o͞o boot	*th* the	pencil,
ä father	ī pie	ô paw,	yo͞o abuse	th thin	atom,
		for	ou out	hw which	circus
				zh vision	ər butter

musket

mu•le•teer | myōol´ lə tîr | —*noun* A person who leads or drives mules.

mus•ket | mŭs´kĭt | —*noun* An old gun with a long barrel. Muskets were used before the invention of the rifle.

mus•tang | mŭs´tăng | —*noun* A small, wild horse of western North America.

muzzle

muz•zle | mŭz´əl | —*noun* The projecting part of an animal's face that includes the nose and mouth; snout.

N

nav•i•ga•tor | năv´ĭ gā´ tər | —*noun* A crew member who plans and directs the course of a ship or an aircraft.

O

op•er•a | ŏp´ər ə | or | ŏp´rə | —*noun* A musical play in which most of the words are sung to orchestral music.

or•bit | ôr´bĭt | —*noun* The path that a man-made satellite or spacecraft takes around the earth.

orbit

or•phan | ôr´fən | —*noun* A child whose parents are dead.

ox•y•gen | ŏk´sĭ jən | —*noun* A gas without color or smell. Oxygen is one of the chemical elements. It makes up one-fifth of the air. People and animals need oxygen to live.

P

pan•el | **păn´** əl | —*noun* A board with instruments or controls for a vehicle or machine.

pa•tri•ot | **pā´** trē ət | or | **pā´** trē ŏt | —*noun* A person who loves, supports, and defends his or her country.

peer | pîr | —*verb* To look closely in order to see something clearly; stare.

pe•o•ny | **pē´** ə nē | —*noun* The large pink, red, or white flowers of a garden plant.

peony

plains | plānz | —*noun* A large, flat area of land without any trees.

plains

post | pōst | —*verb* To put announcements up in a place or in several places for everyone to see.

pow•der horn | **pou´** dər hôrn | —*noun* A container for gunpowder. A powder horn is made of an animal's horn with a cap or stopper at the open end.

powderhorn

Q

quest | kwĕst | —*noun* A search, especially for something valuable.

R

range | rānj | —*noun* A large area of open land on which livestock graze freely.

reb•el | **rĕb´** əl | —*noun* One who rejects authority or fights against it.

ă	pat	ĕ	pet
ā	pay	ē	be
âr	care	ĭ	pit
ä	father	ī	pie
îr	fierce	oi	oil
ŏ	pot	o͝o	book
ō	go	o͞o	boot
ô	paw,	yo͞o	abuse
	for	ou	out
ŭ	cut	ə	ago,
ûr	fur		item,
th	the		pencil,
th	thin		atom,
hw	which		circus
zh	vision	ər	butter

327

reed

reed | rēd | —*noun* A thin strip of wood used in the mouthpiece of certain wind instruments. The reed vibrates when air passes over it and produces a musical tone in the instrument.

re·flec·tion | rē flĕk´shən | —*noun* An image seen through a mirror or piece of transparent glass such as a window.

rep·re·sen·ta·tive | rĕp´rĭ zĕn´tə tĭv | —*noun* A member of the U.S. House of Representatives or of a state legislature.

re·treat | rĭ trēt´ | —*verb* To fall back before an enemy attack; withdraw.

rudder

rev·er·ent | rĕv´ər ənt | —*adjective* Feeling or showing deep respect.

rou·tine | rōō tēn´ | —*adjective* According to the usual or regular way of doing things; ordinary.

rud·der | rŭd´dər | —*noun* Something on a ship or plane that controls direction; guide.

scepter

s **scan** | skăn | —*verb* To look at or examine something closely.

scep·ter | sĕp´tər | —*noun* A rod or staff that is held by a king or queen. It is a symbol of authority.

328

shard | shärd | —*noun* A piece of a substance that is easily broken, such as glass.

shard

shim·mery | shĭm´ ər ē | —*adjective* Anything that is characterized by shining with a flickering or faint light.

snow·shoe | snō´ shoo | —*noun* A light, racket-shaped frame strung with strips of leather or rawhide. Snowshoes are worn under the shoe to keep the feet from sinking into snow.

snowshoe

sou·ve·nir | soo´ və nîr´ | —*noun* Something kept to remember a place, person, or event.

spec·ta·tor | spĕk´ tā tər | —*noun* Someone who watches an event but does not take part in it.

spir·its | spĭr´ ĭts | —*noun* A person's mood or state of mind.

spinning frame

spin·ning frame | spĭn´ ĭng frām | —*noun* A machine that pulls and twists fibers into yarn and winds the yarn on spindles.

spin·ning jen·ny | spĭn´ ĭng jĕn´ ē | —*noun* An early type of spinning machine that had several spindles.

spool | spool | —*noun* A small cylinder made of wood, metal, or plastic. Thread and wire are wound around spools.

ă	pat	ĕ	pet
ā	pay	ē	be
âr	care	ĭ	pit
ä	father	ī	pie
îr	fierce	oi	oil
ŏ	pot	oo	book
ō	go	oo	boot
ô	paw,	yoo	abuse
	for	ou	out
ŭ	cut	ə	ago,
ûr	fur		item,
th	the		pencil,
th	thin		atom,
hw	which		circus
zh	vision	ər	butter

unicycle

sta•bi•liz•er | sta´bə lī´zər | —*noun* A device such as a wing or rudder that steadies an airplane or shuttle while it is flying.

stalk | stôk | —*verb* 1. To walk in a stiff, dignified, or lofty manner. 2. To move in a quiet, cautious way so as not to be noticed; steal after.

stern | stŭrn | —*adjective* Grave and severe.

 thresh | thrĕsh | —*verb* To separate the seeds or grain from a plant by striking or beating it.

tun•nel | tŭn´əl | —*noun* A long passage that is built underground or underwater.

 u•ni•cy•cle | yōō´nĭ sī kəl | —*noun* A vehicle made of a frame built over a wheel and usually propelled by pedals.

 veer | vîr | —*verb* To turn quickly or sharply.

wi•dow | wĭd´ō | —*noun* A woman whose husband has died and who has not remarried.

wine•press | wīn´prĕs | —*noun* A vat in which the juice is pressed from grapes.

winepress

ă pat	ĕ pet	îr fierce	oi oil	ŭ cut	ə ago,
ā pay	ē be	ŏ pot	ŏŏ book	ûr fur	item,
âr care	ĭ pit	ō go	ōō boot	th the	pencil,
ä father	ī pie	ô paw,	yōō abuse	th thin	atom,
		for	ou out	hw which	circus
				zh vision	ər butter